An Ornament for Jewels

An Ornament for Jewels

Love Poems for the Lord of Gods by Vedāntadeśika

TRANSLATIONS WITH COMMENTARY BY

STEVEN P. HOPKINS

OXFORD
UNIVERSITY PRESS
2007

OXFORD
UNIVERSITY PRESS

Oxford University Press, Inc., publishes works that further
Oxford University's objective of excellence
in research, scholarship, and education.

Oxford New York
Auckland Cape Town Dar es Salaam Hong Kong Karachi
Kuala Lumpur Madrid Melbourne Mexico City Nairobi
New Delhi Shanghai Taipei Toronto

With offices in
Argentina Austria Brazil Chile Czech Republic France Greece
Guatemala Hungary Italy Japan Poland Portugal Singapore
South Korea Switzerland Thailand Turkey Ukraine Vietnam

Published by Oxford University Press, Inc.
198 Madison Avenue, New York, New York 10016

www.oup.com

Library of Congress Cataloging-in-Publication Data
Veṅkaṭanātha, 1268–1369.
[Poems. Polyglot. Selections]
An ornament for jewels : love poems for the Lord of Gods /
by Vedāntadeśika ; [edited and translated by] Steven P. Hopkins.
p. cm.
Includes translations from Tamil, Sanskrit, and Maharastri Prakrit.
Includes bibliographical references and index.
ISBN 978-0-19-532639-0; 978-0-19-532640-6 (pbk.)
1. Vishnu (Hindu deity)—Poetry. 2. Religious poetry, Indic—
Translations into English. 3. Veṅkaṭanātha, 1268–1369—
Translations into English.
I. Hopkins, Steven P. II. Title.
PL4758.9.V4255A2 2007
891'.21—dc22 2006053259

9 8 7 6 5 4 3 2 1
Printed in the United States of America
on acid-free paper

For Raimon Panikkar
and
in memory of A. K. Ramanujan
(1929–1993)

And Veṅkaṭeśa, the poet
  composing these verses
of praise
  for You

shines

  a singer of Truth!

—Vedāntadeśika, *Devanāyakapañcāśat* 53

Preface

These translations and this labor to cross over three distinct South Asian languages—Sanskrit, Tamil, and Māhārāṣṭrī Prākrit—into the foreign territories of American English, is the work of over a decade that began with a conversation I had one morning with the late scholar and poet A. K. Ramanujan. We were walking through the streets of Cambridge, Massachusetts, from the Center for the Study of World Religions, where we were both living at the time, to Harvard Yard. I had been giving Raman my own poetry, and was struggling to find the right focus for my dissertation work. He told me then that everything he had thought or written about Indian culture, folklore, or literature began with the act of translation; that this encounter formed a center around which his thinking and his original poetry in English and Kannaḍa always turned. He told me to find a poet, or a body of poetry, preferably in a vernacular language, that I could translate, and in this way I would "keep the poetry" in my own voice, through the voices of other poets, while I pursued my scholarly studies and an academic career. And indeed, reading Ramanujan's remarkable translations from the Tamil of Nammāḻvār and the "classical" Tamil *caṅkam* poetry had first inspired me to study the originals, and to seek my own voice as a translator-poet and scholar. After this conversation, it was not long before I found my poet, Vedāntadeśika, with the help of CSWR colleague and fellow Sanskrit student Tamar Reich. I began then a task I continue today: translating poems from Sanskrit, Tamil, and Prākrit by a fourteenth-century south Indian saint-poet, a creative solitary labor that feeds both the scholar and the poet in me, and remains the center around which my thinking turns.

This encounter with Raman calls to mind a much earlier encounter and walk, this time from South Hall to a classroom on the campus of UC Santa Barbara with Raimon Panikkar. I was not yet even an M.A. student, but was still a poet in a local student community, Isla Vista, who worked in a local coffeehouse. I was beginning, on my own, studies of Catholic, Hindu, and Buddhist traditions, and had begun to sit in on Raimon's classes. I had been deeply struck by my reading of his anthology of Vedic texts, *The Vedic Experience: Mantramañjarī*, the vivid, readable translations of Vedas, Brāhmaṇas, Upaniṣads, and *Gītā*, was eager to learn from the source and quite curious about the possibilities of returning to the university to do graduate studies in religion. I had been giving Raimon my poems, and he had been giving me his articles. I will never forget the gift of one particular offprint, a copy of an article called "*Colligite Fragmenta*: For an Integration of Reality," and most memorably, an overgenerous inscription. This encounter made a deep impression on me, and set me on a course of over twenty years as a student then scholar/professor of comparative religion, from Santa Barbara, to Berkeley, Cambridge, Chennai in south India, and Swarthmore College in Pennsylvania. I continue to correspond with Raimon, who now lives in the hills above Barcelona in the village of Tavertet.

This volume is dedicated to these two mentors and friends, the late A. K. Ramanujan and Raimon Panikkar. It is offered to them with gratitude and thanksgiving.

There are of course many other mentors, scholars, poets, and close friends to thank here—those who helped me bring these translations to light, inspiring and sustaining me through years of slow labor. There is John B. Carman, most attentive of advisors and careful of readers who co-taught a course on bhakti poetry at Harvard with Raman that year long ago; I am also indebted to John Stratton Hawley, Indira Peterson, Mark Juergensmeyer, Vasudha Narayanan, Francis X. Clooney, George Hart, John Cort, Charles Hallisey, Diana Eck, Rachel Fell McDermott, Ann Monius, Leslie Orr, Tracy Coleman, Layne Little, and Pravrajika Vrajaprana for their long support. Special gratitude goes to my dear friend, gifted translator, and scholar of south Indian devotional poetry, Archana Venkatesan, whose infectious enthusiasm for these translations has been of particular support to me in recent years when my academic responsibilities have threatened to overwhelm both me and this project.

Gratitude also to poet friends John Allen Cann, Kerry Tomlinson, and Jonah Bornstein: I hope these translations read like poetry in English. And to Tori, whose music shines a carnivalesque light on everything I do, even on these formal academic pages: *bonfires of fragrant henna and the weeping white keys.*

In south India I will always be deeply grateful to the late S. S. Janaki, former director of the Kuppuswami Shastri Research Institute, Mylapore, Chennai. Professor Janaki patiently read with me selections from an unedited Sanskrit commentary on one of Vedāntadeśika's *stotras*, and first suggested to me that I shape my reading around specific shrines and their images. She also put me in touch with Professor M. Narasimhachary of the Department of Vaishnavism and S. Padmanabhan of the Department of Sanskrit, University of Madras. Professor Padmanabhan's bibliographical suggestions did much to further my research. Dr. Janaki also originally arranged for me to work with Professor R. N. Sampath—former curator at the Government Oriental Manuscripts Library, and professor of Sanskrit, Presidency College, Madras—who, from the very beginning, patiently read with me the Sanskrit, Tamil, and Prākrit poetry that forms the core of this book. I will always be grateful to Professor V. Varadachari of the French Institute of Indology, Pondicherry, and Professor K.K.A. Venkatachari of the Ananthacharya Indological Research Institute, Bombay, who helped provide me with texts and deepened my sense of the inter- and intrasectarian contexts of these poems. Dance master Śrīmati Nandini Ramani, Carnatic singer Saṅgīta Cuḍāmaṇi R. Vedavalli, Śrīman Āṇḍavan Swāmikaḷ, E. Varatatēcikaṉ of Varadarāja Permāḷ temple, and Krishna Raghavan, in Mylapore, Śrī Raṅgam, Kalyāṇapuram, and Kāñcīpuram, provided me with spiritual and aesthetic sustenance at crucial stages of this work.

I want to thank the Council for International Exchange of Scholars and the J. William Fulbright Foundation for a 1997–1998 Faculty Research Scholarship for South India that enabled me to work with Professor R. N. Sampath in Chennai during the fall of 1997 on final versions of many of the complete translations that form a central part of this book. Since my return from India, I am grateful for a 1998–1999 National Endowment for the Humanities (NEH) Summer Stipend for Research, for Swarthmore College Research Funds during the years 1997–2004, and for a Swarthmore College Becker Fellowship in 2000–2001 during my leave year in Swarthmore and in Sri Lanka, all of which helped me continue work on this book.

My fellow traveler and wife, Adrienne, my power and my love, your *śakti* and your deep *aṉpu* continue to sustain me. As the old Tamil poem says, we mingle, in our lives and in the things we love, "without parting," *cempulap peyal nīr pōla*, "like red earth and pouring rain." As for my son, Evan, he has lived through various stages of this project from the Center for the Study of World Religions, Harvard University, the Montessori School in Besant Nagar, Chennai, to Skidmore College in Saratoga Springs, New York.

Finally, along with the anonymous reviewers for Oxford University Press, New York, whose astute responses to an early version of the manuscript made this a much better book, Oxford assistant editors Julia TerMaat and Daniel Gonzalez, and the finest of copy editors, Margaret Case, I am grateful to Cynthia Read, executive editor at Oxford, whose patience and support over a period of several years has made all the difference.

Contents

Pronunciation of Sanskrit and Tamil Words

In the transliteration of Sanskrit words I have followed the convention of Monier-Williams, *A Sanskrit-English Dictionary* (Oxford University Press, 1899); Tamil words have been transliterated according to the system provided by T. Burrow and M. Emeneau, *A Dravidian Etymological Dictionary* (Oxford University Press, 1966 [1961]) and the *Tamil Lexicon* (University of Madras, 6 vols., 1924–1936). The few exceptions to this rule have to do with overall simplicity and clarity for words most commonly used.

The guide to pronunciation of Tamil words is adapted from Indira Peterson, *Poems to Śiva: The Hymns of the Tamil Saints* (Princeton: Princeton University Press, 1989).

Guide to Pronunciation of Sanskrit Words

VOWELS

The line on top of a vowel indicates that it is long.

a (short) as the *u* in b*u*t
ā (long) as the *a* in f*a*r
i (short) as the *i* in s*i*t
ī (long) as the *ee* in sw*ee*t
u (short) as the *u* in p*u*t

ū (long) as the *oo* in cool
ṛ with a dot is a vowel like the *i* in f*i*rst or *u* in f*u*rther
e is always a long vowel like *a* in m*a*te
ai as the *i* in p*i*le
o is always long as the *o* in pole
au as the *ow* in *ow*l

The *visarga,* two vertically lined points (:) is transliterated into roman as an *ḥ* and sounded like the *h* in loch; e.g., Dhanyāḥ, dhīḥ, katākṣaḥ.

CONSONANTS AND NASALS

k is the same in English as in *k*itten
kh is aspirated
g as in goat
gh is aspirated
c is ch as in *ch*urch or *c*ello
ch is aspirated
j as in *j*ewel
jh is aspirated
ṭ and ḍ are hard when dotted below as in *t*alk and *d*ot
ṭh is the aspirated sound
ḍh is aspirated
ṇ when dotted is a dental; the tongue has to curl back to touch the palate
ṅ as in ki*ng*
ñ is as in si*n*ge
t undotted is a th as in *th*ermal
th is aspirated
d undotted is a soft sound—there is no corresponding English sound, the Russian *da* is the closest
dh is aspirated
p and b are the same as in English
ph and bh are aspirated
ṃ is a nasal sound

There are three sibilants in Skt: s as in song, ṣ as in *sh*ove and a palatal ś which is in between; e.g., Śiva.

Guide to Pronunciation of Tamil Words

VOWELS

a (short) like *u* b*u*t
ā* (long) similar to *a* in f*a*ther
i (short) like *i* in *it*
ī* (long) similar to *ee* in k*ee*p
u (short) like *u* in p*u*t
ū* (long) similar to *oo* in c*oo*p
e (short) like *e* in p*e*t or b*e*nch
ē* (long) similar to *a* in c*a*ke
ai like *i* in p*i*pe
o (short) like the first *o* potato
ō* (long) similar to the *o* in *o*pen or *o*ak
au like the *ow* in f*ow*l

* The asterisked long vowels are purer than their English counterparts and closer to Italian vowels.

CONSONANTS AND NASALS

k (guttural) like the English *k*
the nasal ṅ is used with *k*; e.g., Tirumaṅkai
c (palatal) similar to *ch* in *ch*alk, but unaspirated
the nasal ñ is used with *c*; e.g., Kuṟiñci

The following sounds that have come into Tamil from Sanskrit are also represented by c (palatal): *ś*, pronounced *sh*; and *s*, similar to English *s*; e.g., civaṉ (Śiva), pronounced as *S(h)ivan* or *Sivan.*

ṭ is a retroflex sound, pronounced with the tongue curled back
so that it touches the roof of the mouth
ṇ is the retroflex nasal: Āṇṭāḷ
t (dental) is similar to *t* in French or Italian
the nasal n is used with t; e.g., Pirapantam
p is like the English *p*; the nasal *m* is used with *p*

Tamil consonants are pronounced without the slight aspiration that is characteristic of the pronunciation of similar consonants in English.

SEMIVOWELS

y, r, l, and v are similar to their English counterparts; the *r* is rolled
ḻ is similar to the American r, as in *American* or *first.*
ḷ is pronounced as a retroflex sound

ṟ and ṉ are closer to alveolar sounds than r and the other nasal sounds of Tamil; however ṟ and r are almost indistinguishable in contemporary pronunciation; the combination ṟṟ, as in Tirumurukāṟṟuppaṭai, is pronounced like *tr* in *country.*

Special Rules

At the beginning of a word and between vowels, *c* is pronounced like the English *s.*

Between vowels, *k, ṭ, t,* and *p* are voiced, and pronounced as *g* or *h, ḍ, d,* and *b.*

Following a nasal, *k, c, ṭ, t,* and *p* are voiced, and pronounced as *g, j, ḍ, d or dh,* and *b.*

Thus Pirapantam is pronounced as Pirabandham, Caṅkam as Sangam, akam as aham, Murukaṉ as Murugan, neñcai as nenjai, and pātam as pādam.

Doubled consonants are given full value and held longer: e.g., Kacci (Skt: Kāñcī) is pronounced as *kac(h)c(h)i.*

An Ornament for Jewels

I

Introduction: An Ornament for Jewels

Seeing your lovely body whose splendor is made
even more perfect
by each perfect limb,
enjoyed by your beloved wives with unblinking
astonished eyes
and sought out by the jewels and weapons that
adorn it
to increase their own radiance,
my sight O Lord of Gods
is not sated with seeing!

—Vedāntadeśika *Devanāyakapañcāśat* 14

Historically speaking, we know very little about Veṅkaṭanātha or Veṅkaṭeśa, the saint-poet, philosopher, scholar, and logician later known as Vedāntadeśika. Scraps of material testimonies; the witness of a young Telugu prince; some signature verses, panegyrics, and chronicles; an inscription on the walls of Śrīraṅgam praising the feats of a brahman general—bits and pieces of this famous teacher from humble Tūppul with his magnificent epithets. But there are stories, many stories, and a body of work praised and cited by his fourteenth-century contemporaries, chanted in temple rituals, memorized up to the present day—layers of a community's composite of images and experiences.

For the purpose of introducing this book, I begin with a set of stories taken from the sacred biographies (the "Splendors" or *Prabhāvams*) and their evocation of experiences that shape core religious emotions of Veṅkaṭeśa's south Indian tradition. As we will see, these biographies read rather like folktales, popular narratives meant to instruct and inform but also to inspire devotion; they are filled with the conventionally miraculous, themes and motifs common to tales around the world, events and actions that lift Veṅkaṭeśa out of the merely mundane sphere of a great Indian philosopher to that of an almost semidivine figure who himself becomes the focus of religious emotions and cultic veneration.[1]

Narrative and Experience

In true "once upon a time" fashion, his birth was miraculous. His mother had dreams, prophetic dreams that led her and her husband to travel from their home village of Tūppul near Kāñcīpuram to the sacred hill-shrine Tirumālai, to pray to Vishnu who dwelt there as Tirupati, Lord of the Hill, for the gift of a son. One night on the mountain she dreamed that a young boy came to her, asking her to swallow a bell that he held in his hands. That very night the shrine bell at Tirupati was stolen, and the temple priest himself had a dream. In his dream he was told a pious woman would dream of swallowing the bell, and that she would give birth to a remarkable child, an earthly incarnation of the sacred temple bell. Twelve round years later, the stories go, he was born, the temple bell in a baby's small body, the boy named after the god on the hill, Veṅkaṭanātha or Veṅkaṭeśa, "Lord of Veṅkaṭam."

The young boy was prodigious in learning and innate spiritual wisdom: he amazed the old Ācāryas in debate, and eventually took his uncle's place as chief Ācārya (sectarian teacher) at the great temple town of Kāñcī. There he flourished as a talented debater and scholar, a master of scriptures. From there he withdrew for some years to study secret teachings associated with Vishnu's winged mount, Garuḍa, and horse-headed Hayagrīva, whose shrine sat on top of Medicine Herb Hill in the town of Tiruvahīndrapuram. The powers he attained there—scholarly, religious, ritual, magical, and literary—would hold him in good stead over the years, making him a "master of all the arts and sciences," "a lion among poets and philosophers," and giving him the title "Vedāntadeśika" (teacher/master of the Vedānta). And miracles multiply beyond the epithets: he is said to have healed an entire village stricken by plague; to have drawn magic circles on the ground to fight back an attack by supernatural snakes; and with the help of the divine Bird Garuḍa himself, called into form by a mantra, to have destroyed the most potent of serpents sent to vanquish him. In fevered debates with rival Ācāryas from the southern temple town of Śrīraṅgam, he emerged triumphant, holding fast to his "lion-seat" in the city of Kāñcī.

During his middle years, the stories speak of a pilgrimage to the north. Using purely literary journeys that are tucked into various poems, including one of his *sandeśa-kāvyas* or "messenger poems" (the *Haṃsasandeśa*) and one allegorical drama, the *Saṅkalpasūryodaya* (The Dawn of Ritual Resolve), the biographies tell of Veṅkaṭeśa's travel to Banaras and the holy Ganges, to Ayodhyā, Mathurā, Hardvār, places he finds hopelessly corrupted by priests who value only money and have forgotten the teachings and the proper rituals. In his pilgrimage south, like Rāma's "messenger goose" of the *Haṃsasandeśa*, he catches the sweet scent downwind of the blue Vindhya mountains, drinks in and praises in vivid poetry the land, the rivers and the pearl-beds of the deep south, the lovely women of Andhra and Karṇātaka, lakes, temple tanks, and holy shrines of the whole southern country, then finally, after healing a young Vijayanagar princess who was possessed by a demon, and being unsuccessfully wooed for the court and its patronage by the court-philosopher Vidyāraṇya, he comes home to Kāñcī, whose great gods, Vishnu and Śiva, in native, indigenous harmony, signal each other from their temple towers, mingling on the clear air the sounds of their bells and the odors of their lustrations.

His later years, say the narratives, are spent in turbulent debate in Śrīraṅgam. He is said to have endured the taunting and abuse of rival Ācāryas: sandals strung over his doorway—a most disgusting insult—a boycott of his father's funeral rites, the hiding of gold in his daily grain rations in the hopes that he would accidentally touch what he had vowed never to touch. But what follows in the story is far worse than sectarian debate, and brings the Ācāryas together: Veṅkaṭeśa is associated with a narrative that is popular in various temple tales: the Muslim "sack of Śrīraṅgam," the "invasion that took 12,000 heads."

As Muslims advanced on Śrīraṅgam, Veṅkaṭeśa stayed behind while his Ācārya rival and friend, Piḷḷai Lokācārya, escaped north to Tirupati with the temple's festival icons. As the army began pressing into the town and into the heart of the temple complex, Veṅkaṭeśa walled up the main stone images of the shrine, and after hiding under a pile of dead bodies, finally fled to safety with a copy of a precious manuscript and headed for exile in Mysore. After long exile in Mysore and in the temple town of Melkote, he eventually returned to Śrīraṅgam on the heals of a successful campaign to retake the city led by the brahman general Gopaṇārya. It is there, in Śrīraṅgam, that he is said to have lived out his years, putting final touches on his vast work of philosophical commentary, logic, original treatises, and poetry in three languages, Tamil, Sanskrit, and Māhārāṣṭrī Prākrit. Indeed, his verses in Sanskrit to the victorious brahman general still grace the inner temple walls of Śrīraṅgam.[2]

Ritual Experience

To understand the poems translated in this book, their place in a tradition's self-understanding, we must know these stories, along with scraps of material histories, recognizing basic themes of a narrative, often drawn, as we have seen, from images in the poems themselves. Yet biographical folktale motifs are hardly enough. We must also understand certain structures of shaped experience within the narratives, constructions of idealized religious emotions bound up with an experience of temples, temple spaces, and above all, images (mobile and immobile icons, paintings) of a deity who is, though transcendent, thought also to be alive in a material way before the eyes of the devotee. Such experience and such emotions are embraced by the rich Sanskrit term *anubhava*, "relish," "enjoyment," "experience," used in the poems, commentaries, and the narratives. Here ritual action—cult—joins with story to help contextualize the poems of this philosopher-saint and teacher.[3]

Taking one moment at random from Veṅkaṭeśa's poems, we must imagine it is May, the month of Vaikāsi, in Little Kāñcīpuram. The mobile image of Varadarāja Perumāḷ is carried into the inner courtyard of the temple as the devotees line up for *darśana*, a devotional viewing of the deity, when they can see and also be seen by the god. When the crowd of "fortunate ones" (*dhanyāḥ*) approaches the tall icon, stripped of all its ornaments, its jewels and silks and embossed silver, but for the yellow waistcloth and streaks of vermilion paste on its forehead, its chest and feet, some begin to weep uncontrollably. Veṅkaṭeśa the saint-poet shapes these powerful feelings, what he himself coins in a phrase in Tamilized Sanskrit as the "spontaneous overflow of emotion" (*anupava parivāhamāka*), into vivid concise verses:

> Those few blessed god-lovers
> their thin small bodies swelling in wave after wave of ecstasy
>   hair standing on end
> their bud-like eyes welling with thick tears,
>   O Varada,
> are ornaments in your assembly.
> Their hearts made firm by an inner humility,
>   they sweeten your feet . . .

Here living, vulnerable human bodies come in contact with a seemingly alive, though impassible and perfected divine body in the heart of the temple and in the heart of the *pūjā* or ritual veneration of the god. Such a *pūjā* for the saint-poet is an elaborately layered experience; it is about formal prestations, offerings and formal exchange of "blessings," but it is also always the site of devotional vision: though the concrete site of the poem is a crowded temple sanctum, the poet imagines himself an ornament at the feet of the handsome god-king, watching as the god rises at dawn from his royal bed, bearing on his throat the marks of Queen Indirā's gold bangles. This god-king is Vishnu, and she, of many names—Indirā, Śrī, Lakṣmī—Queen and Goddess:

Those few blessed O Varada
  see your dark blue body stripped of ornaments
    and silver armor—
the original model for Elephant Hill,
its blue made deeper blue
   by fragrant *kasturi*.

Bearing O Varada
on your throat the marks of Indirā's gold bracelets
left by her tight embraces
you rise at dawn
  from your serpent bed—
may you always be present in my mind's inner core.[4]

Asymmetry and Intimacy: Devotional Poetics and the Body of God

Icons here are far more than mere pointers to or reminders of their divine referent; rather, they are seen in the eyes of the saint-poet as living "bodies" of the deity, the concentrated form of the godhead in the small space of a precious metal (mobile bronze "festival image," the *utsavamūrti*) or stone figure (the sanctum image or *mūlabera*). In the saint-poet's "devotional eye," to use a phrase of Richard Davis, they are "pieces" of heaven on earth, and in some instances make earth—for the other gods as well as for human devotees—preferable to heaven.[5] In Veṅkaṭeśa's devotional poetics, "holy seeing" (*darśana*)—seeing and being seen *by* God—is the experience of a perfected, transcendental beauty (Tamil: *aḻaku*; Sanskrit: *lāvaṇya,* glowing loveliness) that saves. For Deśika, what we might term the "aesthetic" and "religious" mutually inhere in the vision of the body of god, both on a theoretical and on an experiential level.

This devotional encounter in the sanctum, this seeing and being seen, also points to a structural asymmetry that is critical to our understanding of particular and ideal forms of love in Veṅkaṭeśa's poetry. The poems often enact the dialectic of an unruly, vulnerable, emotionally fragile, volatile, and liquid love (the weepy, horripilating bodies of the "blessed ones"), with the perfected, contained and ideal body of the god, a god who is loving and who is sometimes *in love* with selected devotees, but who is always also in control—a dialectic of the chaos and cosmos of devotion. The texts, and the saint-poet, strive, of course, for that transcendental cosmicized love embodied in the idealized body of Vishnu, a refinement of simple material emotions. At the same time, they valorize, in their conventional emotional overflow (*anubhava parivāha*), the vulnerable human lover, in all his or her extravagance of desire and vulnerability of feeling. We will see this asymmetrical structure in the poet's constant oscillation between the experience of divine presence and absence, intimacy and distance, in verses that move from ecstatic praise of the Lord's proximity to complaint and lament over separation. Such a coexistence of asymmetry and intimacy in love, this willed ambiguity, is most complexly inscribed in Veṅkaṭeśa's literary uses of the *akam* or "interior" love motifs in his Tamil poems, in their conventional female personae and expressive fragile emotions, and in formal *anubhavas*, or stepwise image-rich and sensuous descriptions of the body of Vishnu from head to foot in his Sanskrit and Prākrit lyrics—a motif that holds in tension together the loving particularity and transcendent impassibility of the god.[6]

The Telescope of Experience/Telescope of the Poem

Though commonly, and in the manner of the Provençal troubadour lyric of medieval Europe, each stanza of Veṅkaṭeśa's long poetry sequences is a praise-poem or singular word picture that stands on its own, again and again we are struck by an overall telescoping structure of this experience of *darśana*, emotional beholding, in the poems and in the descriptions in the narratives. In pulsating dynamic rhythm, in a quasi-musical structure of theme and variations, what is far in the mythic past becomes concrete and totally present in the transfigured time and space of the *pūjā* and in the experience (*anubhava*) of the saint-poet who stands there, in front of the temple image. The great god who willed this world into being, who has taken the forms of so many gods—the hero Rāma, Krishna, the lover of the cowgirls, butter thief, killer of King Kaṃsa—who has for millennia, long before this age, defeated so many enemies of the earth and who is also identified as *Brahman*, the impersonal "ground of being," has taken on a beautiful body of bronze and gold or a mysterious image of black stone, to stand here before the saint-poet, now, *in this very place*, for the sake of the devotees. And the god stood and still stands not only in "this" place, but also, as the poet rediscovers (after forgetting) over and over again, in his own heart.

These are the three spatial and temporal worlds—cosmic, terrestrial, interior/individual—traced in each of Veṅkaṭeśa's poems. They are made present, to use the coinage of Raimon Panikkar, in the "tempiternal present" of *darśana* in the shrine or simply in the reading/recitation/chanting/singing of the praise-poem that reproduces, in literary form, this experience for the reader/reciter/singer.[7] We are able to gaze, simultaneously, through the ground glass of the praise-poem, at eons of past, present, and even future time and space. As an astonishing final realization, built into the poem itself, we are made to realize that all this, however apart from us, is also, paradoxically, within us.

I might also mention here that this pattern reproduces, within the sacred (oral/aural/audial) space of the poem, the slow physical progress of a devotee as she (or he) approaches the temple. Noting the landscape around it—marked with shrines of ancillary gods, the shrine to the nine planets, the holy river and sacred tree, shrines related to various place-narratives of the temple—she works her way from the exterior courtyards and their shrines, step by step, *pradakṣiṇa*, (with her right side facing the temple), until she enters the darkest, smallest, and often the oldest part of the temple complex, the so-called *garbha gṛha*, the "womb-house" of the temple where the central sanctum image "stands." It is in this smallest, most spiritually condensed place that the saint-poet, gazing at the image of the living heart of the temple complex, experiences that all of this—the temple spaces, the gods and goddesses, the shrines, and even this god that she gazes upon—is also in the heart.

In the individual afterword to each poem I will note this recurring three-fold telescoping structure as it unfolds in Veṅkaṭeśa's literary art, often within each verse as well as in the sequences—the *stotras* and *prabandhams*—as a whole. I will also note the various registers of asymmetry and intimacy present in the literary and theological structures of certain individual verses, as well as in the overarching framework of entire cycles.

Love Poems for the Lord of Gods at Tiruvahīndrapuram

One of the most powerful of all places of divine presence for Veṅkaṭeśa is on a hill near an ancient Serpent Well, where the form of Vishnu as the Lord of Gods, Devanāyaka at Tiruvahīndrapuram (Sacred Town of the King of Serpents), dwells in icon form. Veṅkaṭeśa's sacred narratives speak of this place as a kind of interregnum place of peace and spiritual development. It is also the place associated in the biographies with important ritual initiations. Long ago, before the hard debates at Kāñcī and Śrīraṅgam, before the painful morning when his wife found the gold pieces in the bowl of grain, and he made her throw each precious glittering piece in the gutter, it was at Tiruvahīndrapuram where he was taught the mantras, the spells of power, where he sat at the feet of Lord Hayagrīva and learned the rituals. And this was where, just as he was about to return to Kāñcīpuram, in dead of night, the Lord of Tiruvahīndrapuram came to him—a temple image taken animate form, walking on the red road like a man—and told him not to leave before he had composed for him "in his own words" what was sung in the "old Veda." Veṅkaṭeśa then returned to the village and praised Devanāyaka, the Lord of Tiruvahīndrapuram, in Tamil, his mother-tongue; in Prākrit, the tongue of southern singers and the child-goddess Sarasvatī; and in his own vivid Sanskrit. It is this god and this icon that he praises in his poems as the equal of its own jewels: even more, Veṅkaṭeśa says, this body of Vishnu is itself an ornament for the jewels.

These poems and the narratives that surround them make up this volume—these complex literary acts of devotion and offering to Devanāyaka Swāmi at Tiruvahīndrapuram that we seek to understand and to read in American English. But before I touch upon the themes of sources, structure, and translation, we still need to fill in, beyond the portraits in the sacred narratives and the thematic structures of the poems themselves, the social/historical and religious background of the work of this saint-poet of Tūppul.

Veṅkaṭeśa: A "Lion among Poets and Philosophers"

The medieval south Indian saint-poet, theologian, and philosopher Veṅkaṭanātha or Veṅkaṭeśa (ca. 1268–1369), commonly known by his epithet Vedāntadeśika ("Preceptor of the Vedānta"), is one of the most important brahman Ācāryas (sectarian preceptors) of the Śrīvaiṣṇava community of south India. This particular Vaiṣṇava community worships a personal god in the form of Lord Vishnu, one of the high gods of Hindu tradition, along with his consort-goddess Śrī or Lakṣmī.[8] The Śrīvaiṣṇava community, which first developed around the tenth to eleventh centuries, claims the Tamil poems of the Āḻvārs, especially those of the saint-poet Nammāḻvār, as equal in status to the Sanskrit Veda. Long after Veṅkaṭeśa's death, he was claimed as the founding Ācārya of the Vaṭakalai or "northern" school of Śrīvaiṣṇavism, centered in the ancient holy city of Kāñcīpuram in northern Tamil Nadu. Veṅkaṭeśa's early association with the northern city of Kāñcī would be a significant source of his broad learning, his polylinguism, and what might be termed his cosmopolitanism. For Kāñcīpuram, even before the time of Veṅkaṭeśa, had long been associated with multiple religious communities—Buddhist, Jain, Hindu—and a decidedly cosmopolitan atmosphere. The city had deep roots in transregional brahminical Sanskrit learning, though it also fostered the development of regional cosmopolitan literatures, most notably in Pāli and Tamil.

Along with working in three major languages of his southern tradition—Sanskrit, Tamil, and Māhārāṣṭrī Prākrit—Veṅkaṭeśa was a master of many genres of philosophical prose and poetry. He wrote long ornate religious poems (*kāvyas*) in Sanskrit; a Sanskrit allegorical drama (*nāṭaka*); long religious lyric hymns (*stotras* and *prabandhams*) in Sanskrit, Māhārāṣṭrī Prākrit, and in Tamil; as well as commentaries and original works of philosophy, theology, and logic in Sanskrit and in a hybrid combination of the Sanskrit and Tamil languages called *maṇipravāḷa* ("jewels and coral"). Tradition ascribes to him the resounding epithets of *kavitārkikasiṃha*, "a lion among poets and philosophers (or logicians)," and *sarvatantrasvatantra*, "master of all the arts and sciences." Such epithets embody a certain spirit of creative cultural and linguistic synthesis. Veṅkaṭeśa was master of all "tantras" (this term embraces multiple genres of texts); he was also both a *kavi* (a master poet) and a *tārkika* (logician/debater/philosopher). Tensions and complementarities between poet and philosopher, the devotional lyric and theological prose, are enacted within the same person.

Veṅkaṭeśa's devotional poetry combines in a dynamic way the local/regional literary prestige of Tamil with the panregional aesthetic prestige and power of Sanskrit (with Māhārāṣṭrī as Middle Indo-Āryan literary spice). His writings expand the linguistic field of south Indian devotion beyond the normative claims either of Sanskrit or Tamil devotional texts, and his language choices embrace both the singularity of Sanskrit as divine "primordial tongue" and the subordinate but equally divine claims of his mother tongue, Tamil.

Veṅkaṭeśa in South Indian Bhakti Literature

Any reading of Veṅkaṭeśa's poetic work in Sanskrit, Tamil, and Prākrit must include an account of the religiohistorical and literary streams in which it is situated and of which it is, in great measure, a late flowering. Such an account must begin with the extraordinary rise of Śaiva and Vaiṣṇava devotional movements in the deep south during the reign of the Pallavas of Kāñcī and the Pāṇḍiyas of Madurai.[9]

Between the sixth and ninth centuries C.E. there occurred in south India what A. K. Ramanujan has called "a great, many-sided shift in Hindu culture and sensibility."[10] This shift consisted in the rise of a new kind of religious devotion (*bhakti*), rooted in the renewal of an activist sectarian temple cult and the emotionally charged Tamil poetry of the Śaiva Nāyaṉārs (Masters) and the Vaiṣṇava Āḻvārs.[11] This by no means marks the beginnings of Indian bhakti per se. Highly developed forms of devotional worship and literature had of course been around for quite some time, as widespread among Buddhist and Jain communities as they were among Hindus.[12] Moreover, bhakti as a full-blown spiritual path linked to certain meditative and ritual practices had received its Hindu apotheosis centuries before Pallava times in the Sanskrit *Bhagavad Gītā*, the *Harivaṃśa*, the still-mysterious plays of Bhāsa, and the early Purāṇas.[13] What Ramanujan refers to, however, as a "shift" in the south during the Pallava and Pāṇḍiya dynasties meant bhakti with an ideological difference. Both god and devotee were made to speak in a distinctly new idiom, and with a Tamil accent. This shift in the poetics of devotion offered an alternative form of sacredness to the dominant one shaped by Jains and Buddhists before the seventh century.

Before the advent of this new Hindu devotional orthodoxy, according to Burton Stein, in the centuries between the period of classical Tamil literature (first to third centuries C.E.) and the rise of the Pallavas, "the zenith of Jaina and Buddhist influence in South India was achieved."[14] This was the period of the so-called "Kaḷabhra interregnum" when nonpeasant warrior-caste peoples had wrested power away from the lowland peasant population.[15] This period also witnessed the growing influence of northern Āryan cults. It was a time of great cultural pluralism, social change, and yet relative peace in the south. For it appears, as Stein notes, that "these cults coexisted peacefully with each other and with indigenous forms of religion and that the Jaina and Buddhist sects of South India were as successful as Śaivite and Vaishnavite sects in winning the allegiance of leaders in South Indian society."[16] By the seventh century, as several inscriptions and the accounts of the Chinese pilgrim Hsüang-tsang attest, the Jains seemed to have had the advantage over the Buddhists and Hindus; they were most favored by the dominant urban, nonpeasant warrior classes that controlled the plains.[17] During the seventh and eighth centuries this period of peaceful coexistence came to an end, as did the dominance of urban warriors.[18]

The very symbols of the end of peaceful coexistence, and of "the bitterness and violence" of the sectarian controversies that erupted with the rise of the bhakti cults, are in Śaiva sources on the conversions of kings. The Pallava monarch Mahendravarman I, said to have once been a persecutor of Śaivas, turned his vehemence on the Jains at his conversion to Śaivism.[19] An even more infamous story, for which there is no solid material evidence, is told in Śaiva literary sources such as the twelfth-century *Periyapurāṇam* of Cēkkiḻār and in a series of vivid frescoes on the *maṇḍapam* walls of the Mīṇākṣī temple tank. It is the story of the newly converted Pāṇḍiya king of Madurai.

First a Jain, Sundarapāṇṭiya is said to have been converted to Śaivism by the Nāyaṉār child saint-poet Campantar. Presumably on the saint's urging (or without his resistence), the newly converted king had 8,000 Jains impaled on stakes—an event (a legend rather)—that is still celebrated in an annual festival at Mīṇākṣī Temple in Madurai.[20] Later, in the eighth century, the Vaiṣṇava king Nandivarman II Pallavamalla carried out systematic persecutions of Buddhists and Jains, inspired in great measure by the fervor of the bhakti revival. It is about this time, according to a later hagiographical tradition, that the Vaiṣṇava saint-poet Tirumaṅkaiyāḻvār (Parakāla) is said to have plundered the Buddhist *vihāra* at Nāgapaṭṭinam and melted down the golden Buddha image to cover the walls of Śrīraṅgam with gold.[21]

Throughout this period, the Śaiva and Vaiṣṇava Tamil saints either reconsecrated or virtually sang into existence a complex network of sacred places, temples, and shrines that would grow in size and political influence by royal patronage throughout the next four centuries.[22] The saints in both communities hailed from all social strata, from brahman to untouchable. Their poems, though of mixed genres, are generally simple and direct in style; they are marked by their stress on Tamil as a sacred tongue equal to the Veda.[23] The poems combine, in an original way, emotional directness and a vocabulary imbued with cultic terminology and imagery that witness their use in and influence by esoteric and public temple ritual.[24] Some of these poems, especially those of the Vaiṣṇava Āḻvārs, self-consciously use the conventions of classical Tamil love poetry to describe the passionate (even erotic) relationship between devotee and deity.[25]

The Āḻvārs' First Ācāryas and Veṅkaṭeśa's Cosmopolitan Age

There began in the period of the Āḻvārs what would become throughout Cōḻa times a more and more intimate alliance between brahmans, their ritually dependent kings, and high-caste, nonbrahman peasants. The Hindu devotional movements swept the plains and swiftly won over converts from their nearest competition, the popular Jain goddess (*yakṣiṇī*) cults that had held sway up until the eighth century.[26] The urban, nonpeasant Jain and Buddhist communities never recovered the ideological, economic, or religious power they had enjoyed in the south before the seventh century.

The next period is marked by a more self-conscious brahman consolidation of power and of intellectual and institutional synthesis. Whereas the Āḻvārs emphasized solely the regional Tamil tongue in their hymns, the early Vaiṣṇava Ācāryas or sectarian teachers, such as Yāmunācārya, Kūreśa (Kūrattāḻvāṉ), and Parāśara Bhāṭṭar, active from the tenth century on, wrote Sanskrit hymns (*stotras*) in praise of specific icons of Vishnu modeled after the vivid Tamil of the Āḻvārs.[27] As Nancy Nayar has convincingly shown, the poems of Ācāryas Kūreśa and Parāśara Bhāṭṭar are filled with allusions to the Tamil of the Āḻvārs (*the drāviḍa veda*) in their devotional imagery and use of place names.[28] The Ācāryas, addressing a thoroughly bilingual audience, made various attempts, in Friedhelm Hardy's words, to "achieve a reconciliation between brahminical orthodoxy, the Pāñcarātra and typically Southern factors like the mysticism of the Āḻvārs and their belief in a personal absolute."[29] We see here the beginnings of a tradition of the "Dual" or "Ubhaya Vedānta," the "jewels-and-coral" synthesis that reached its acme in the development of Śrīvaiṣṇava *maṇipravāḷa*.[30] This era of Rāmānuja and the early Ācāryas produced both commentarial and original works; it saw the composition of voluminous theological commentaries on Tamil hymns as well as the composition of sophisticated Sanskrit *stotras* that combined classical Sanskrit poetics with the emotional bhakti of the Āḻvārs. From here, we move on to the divisive but religiously rich centuries during and after the time of Veṅkaṭeśa.

Veṅkaṭeśa's life spans the waning of the Cōḻa dynasty and the beginnings of Vijayanagar, where the expansion of the Telugu warriors into the Tamil land created a new set of alliances. His rich poetic and philosophical output in Tamil, Sanskrit, Māhārāṣṭrī Prākrit, and *maṇipravāḷa*, as well as his conscious synthesis of regional and panregional idioms, accurately reflects the religious and ideological pluralism of the emerging Vijayanagar empire. In Veṅkaṭeśa we also have a living embodiment of a twin process active during this period as well: the revival of Sanskrit textual production in courtly and religious circles in an age also defined by forces of vernacularization.[31] We find in Veṅkaṭeśa's time a cultural atmosphere analogous in its cosmopolitanism and interreligious and interlinguistic contacts to that of the still-mysterious Kaḷabhra interregnum—but this time under Hindu rule and a peasant-Telugu warrior alliance.[32]

In a synthesis that reflects his time, Veṅkaṭeśa moves the "Tamil tradition" of passionate devotion forward from its local and regional focus to a broader, translocal context through his Sanskrit and Prākrit compositions; but at the same time he composes his own original Tamil poems that expand and affirm Tamil literary tradition, and its own regional ambitions as a divine tongue of saint-poets, without being diluted or muted by Sanskrit.

Poems for the Lord of Gods: Devanāyaka's Shrine as Microcosm

My earlier study, *Singing the Body of God*, focused its textual analyses on Veṅkaṭeśa's praise-poems to three iconic forms of Vishnu, *mūrtis* or *arcāvatāras*: the shrine and icons of Varadarājaperumāḷ in the northern temple town of Kāñcīpuram; those of Lord Devanāyaka at the small village of Tiruvahīndrapuram near the southeastern coastal town of Cuddalore (Kaṭalūr); and finally, the shrine and icons of Lord Raṅganātha at Śrīraṅgam, a temple complex that became, by the tenth century, the most important southern center of power in Veṅkaṭeśa's community. As I argued in some detail in *Singing the Body of God*, and touched on above, these poems are complex theological and philosophical constructions in lyric/hymnic form, each unfolding Veṅkaṭeśa's full theological vision in an individual way suited to its particular sacred object or image and place.

This volume of translations focuses on such poems written to only one form of Vishnu, that of Devanāyaka, the Lord of Gods at Tiruvahīndrapuram. The poems written at this sacred place, in character with others of the same genre—though emphasizing a certain "emotionalism" toward this form of Vishnu—form a kind of microcosm of the saint-poet's work, and compress within their compass most of the central themes in Veṅkaṭeśa's devotional poetics. These include the union of intellect and emotion; the idea of a "beauty that saves," a certain theological aesthetics; the dynamic, sometimes contrary relationship between poetry and philosophy (with poetry adding dimensions of fluidity to the philosopher's formulations); and the play of divine absence and radical presence in the sacred place, in images and in temple ritual (*pūjā*). Moreover, the poems to this Lord of Gods at Tiruvahīndrapuram form more than a thematic microcosm; they also embrace all three of the poet's working languages, forming a linguistic microcosm as well.

Veṅkaṭeśa wrote praise-poems for Devanāyaka in Sanskrit, Tamil, and Māhārāṣṭrī Prākrit, for good reason—indeed, as the place-legend describes, by divine command. One of the core stories of the place-legend of Tiruvahīndrapuram describes the moment when these poems—and this self-conscious work—were born. Veṅkaṭeśa was heading out of town, on the road back to Kāñcīpuram, when the Lord of Gods, Vishnu at Tiruvahīndrapuram shrine, came to him in the dark of night as he slept near the river Peṇṇai. I have already noted how the god commanded the poet not to leave the town and the shrine until he had sung "in his own words" what is sung about Him "in the old Veda." One of the concluding verses of these poems makes it clear what his "own words" were to be: praises in the "old tongue," Sanskrit, in "charming, heart-warming" Prākrit, and in "pure, graceful Tamil."[33]

Thus this selection, by focusing not only on full translations of individual poems, themselves coherent theological "visions" in verse, but also on poems written in praise of a single god in a single place, will give the reader a sense of Veṅkaṭeśa's whole project, his linguistic, emotional, and intellectual registers. It will have the advantage of focus and literary elegance; like the remembered world of Proust's Combray in the taste of madeleine dipped in tea, or his experience of the sea at Balbec, the aquarium windows of the Grand Hotel and its "frieze" of girls distilled in the astringent feel of a starched napkin, and like Blake's World in a Grain of Sand, we taste and see, in this one particular place, and in this one particular form of Vishnu, various protean forms and powers of the divine, and trace a veritable summa of theological, philosophical, and literary designs.

These hymns of Veṅkaṭeśa to the beautiful icon-bodies of Devanāyaka at Tiruvahīndrapuram both reflect his rootedness in the icon-based poems of the Āḻvār and Ācārya traditions and express some of the most emotional aspects of Veṅkaṭeśa's own devotional poetics. In such poems that "sing the body of God" we can most vividly see his distinctive contributions to the south Indian Vaiṣṇava tradition he inherited. Both similarities and differences with regard to Āḻvār and Ācārya bhakti are most clearly inscribed in these particular kinds of hymns. Moreover, such icons in "beloved places" inspire some of Veṅkaṭeśa's finest poetry.

Sources, Structure, and Translation

Sources

I will not reproduce here my detailed analyses in *Singing the Body of God* of the various editions of Veṅkaṭeśa's Sanskrit and Prākrit *stotras* and Tamil *prabandhams*, or the significance of dates, particular commentator/editors, and provenance to the "Tamil consciousness" movements in the Tamil Nadu of the 1930s and 1940s. I refer the reader to the full-length study for textual, linguistic, and historiographical issues.[34] For the purpose of this thematic collection of translations, I want to simply make mention of my basic sources for these poems to Devanāyaka Swāmi. I have utilized throughout two editions of Veṅkaṭeśa's poems: the *Śrīdeśikastotramālā, uraiyuṭaṉ*, edited with a modern Tamil commentary and word gloss of V. N. Śrī Rāmatēcikācāryar for the Sanskrit and Prākrit poems, and Rāmatēcikācāryar's edited collection of the "Deśika Prabandham" with "simple" Tamil commentary, individual word glosses, indices of first lines, and detailed glossaries (*Śrītēcikappirapantam, uraiyuṭaṉ*), for the Tamil poems. Although many of the Sanskrit *stotras* collected by Rāmatēcikācāryar have a rich liturgical history at temples associated with Veṅkaṭeśa, or have roots in separate manuscript traditions, most of the Tamil *prabandhams* are extracted from Veṅkaṭeśa's longer prose *rahasyas* ("secrets") or elaborate esoteric texts enumerating points of Śrīvaiṣṇava doctrine. The poems collected in this volume, including the *Gopālaviṃśati* to Devanāyaka as the pan-Indian Krishna, Tirumaṅkaiyāḻvār's decad of verses in praise of Tiruvahīndrapuram, and the Tamil *prabandhams* (the *Mummaṇikkōvai* and the *Navamaṇimālai*) all have liturgical significance at the temple of Devanāyaka Swāmi. The Tamil *prabandhams*, along with the Sanskrit *stotra Devanāyakapañcāśat*, are chanted at Veṅkaṭeśa's feast days. As the first part of this introduction expresses in a lyrical mode, these praises of this "body of god," a very "ornament for the jewels," are far more than metaphorical products of religious imagination alone: they have a concrete referent, a material, cultic center of gravity, an icon in the temple, around which swirls a plethora of metaphors and emotions, of dissembling similes and extravagant hyperbole. We will have the opportunity to explore the significance of this in more detail in the afterwords to each poem.

The Structure of the Book

This collection consists of complete translations of five long poems of Veṅkaṭeśa: two from the Tamil, *Mumaṇikkōvai* and *Navamaṇimālai*, and two, *Devanāyakapañcāśat* and *Gopālaviṃśati*, from the Sanskrit. Selected verses from these poems are analyzed in the larger study, as luminous details that condense various semantic registers and theological colors of the whole, but here the reader can encounter these individual verses set within the larger canvas of the entire visionary cycle. I also include a full translation of the Prākrit *Acyutaśatakam*, also selected in *Singing the Body of God*. Finally, I conclude, for comparative reasons, with a translation of the only praise of Tiruvahīndrapuram written by a poet of the Tamil Āḻvār generation, Tirumaṅkaiyāḻvār's luminous decad of verses for Devanāyaka from the *Periyatirumoḻi* (III: 1–10). Each poem forms a chapter in itself, and has its own individual short afterword (or foreword in the case of Tirumaṅkai), along with detailed linguistic and thematic notes and commentary. The ultimate goal of this volume is to focus on Veṅkaṭeśa's remarkable poems themselves, their argument in images in an anthology setting, set side by side with sister poems in the other languages, in translations that seek to bring the Sanskrit, Tamil, and Prākrit originals into readable American English verse forms.

At the Edge of the Woods: Thoughts about Translation

In the context of fidelity in translation, I never fail to think of the great *ficción* of Borges about Pierre Menard, "Author of the Quixote." Borges, as usual, is one of the best tonics for those who take themselves too seriously. Menard's desire was not to compose another *Quixote*, but to compose *the* Quixote; to get at the heart of what Cervantes himself meant in his great seventeenth-century work, to write the Quixote *through the experiences of Pierre Menard*, "to produce a number of pages" as the narrator of the *ficción* tells us, "which coincided—word for word and line for line—with those of Miguel de Cervantes."[35] As absurd as this may seem, here is a temptation that haunts every translator and translation (the act that, by its strange determined nature, takes us over). We seek, though we know that this is impossible, and perhaps not at all desirable, some kind of radical transparency—in rhythm of phrasing, alliteration, meter, conceit—a moment of almost mystical kinship, where two languages meet to such an extent that, say, Veṅkaṭeśa—or Kabīr, Aimé Césaire, Arnaut Daniel, Biatritz de Dia, Proust—*becomes* American English. Borges's fabula about Pierre Menard goes several steps further; it pushes the limits of this desire for fidelity, containing the lovely irony that, finally, after Herculean labors and innumerable drafts, thousands of ripped up or burned handwritten pages, Menard's Quixote and the Cervantes text were indeed "identical," though the narrator remarks that the twentieth-century French novelist/critic Menard's text (in flawless seventeenth-century Castilian) is "almost infinitely richer." I sometimes laugh, thinking of this, after working long hours on Veṅkaṭeśa's Tamil, Prākrit, or Sanskrit verses: the most nearly perfect "translation," the most accurate "reading," will be to have labored with draft on draft of English, only, after so many missteps, to arrive "back" at the Tamil, Prākrit, or Sanskrit text.

But practically speaking my goals, and those of most translators, are far less ambitious than Menard's; they are more immediate and practical, though for that no less critical for my immediate context, the rather checkered history of translations from South Asian languages.

I seek to avoid here what Hank Heifetz has called the "tradition of the bad" in translation from South Asian languages, particularly from Sanskrit, a style he refers to as "Indologese," a blend of the artificial and archaic with the obsessively literal, translations salt-and-peppered by parentheses and variant phrases that obscure the fact that the originals are vivid, powerful, elegant poems.[36] As a scholar of South Asian Religion, Languages, and Literatures, as well as a poet who has written and published poems that speak in my own American English voice of south Indian landscapes, of people I have known, of images and forms of deities in various temples in Tamil Nadu, I attempt a double task here: to provide translations that are both scholarly—informed by and accurate to the original—and readable in English. I trust that my translations will repay close scrutiny and rereading, and that they will read well aloud; but also it is my hope that, through the detailed notes provided for individual verses, phrases, or words, with sometimes extensive quotations from the original texts, the reader will get a sense of the originals. In this foreign terrain, the ideational content, can be rather easily transferred from language to language; but I hope to convey in the sometimes rather idiomatic English of the translations—through alliteration, internal rhyme, an unusually long-limbed line with little punctuation, and at times the clipped, uneven spacing on the page—a bodily sense of the rhythms, the line, the internal semantic and syntactic movement (breath line and measure) of the original. It is my hope that, to make good translations, one does not need to be so free as to obliterate any sense of an "original." I am confident that one can compose a "new" English poem that creatively mediates the message and linguistic textures of its "original."

This is a difficult balance to strike. As Paul Blackburn, the great translator of Occitan (Old Provençal) troubadour lyrics, noted some years ago in an interview:

> [Question:] What is the difference between free and strict, literal translation? Between free translation and outright adaptation? [Answer:] Very often readability. Strict translation usually makes for stiff English, or forced and un-english rhythms. Outright adaptation is perfectly valid if it makes a good, modern poem. Occasionally, an adaptation will translate the spirit of the original to better use than any other method: at other times, it will falsify the original beyond measure. Much depends upon the translator (also upon the reader).[37]

As the reader will see from the notes, these are far from "free" translations or "adaptations," and I do not aspire to Walter Benjamin's fascinating but perilous Kabbalistic evocation of the "task of the translator" as releasing "in his own language that pure language which is under the spell of another, to liberate the language imprisoned in a work in his re-creation of that work."[38] As translations, these English poems are not, again to use the vivid vocabulary of Benjamin, "at the center of the language forest": they are, of necessity, "on the outside facing the wooded ridge," calling into the woods of the original languages "without entering"; they aim, in Benjamin's words, "at that single spot where the echo is able to give, in its own language, the reverberation of the work in the alien one."[39] These are echoes, verbal reverberations, of the originals, and so are derivative, secondary, loyal to their models in various ways that sometimes stretch the norms of English syntax, but also they seek to be poems in English that stand on the page as poetry in their own right. In George Steiner's formulation, these translations are echoes, indeed, but echoes that hope to enrich, far more than "shadow and inert simulacrum."[40]

Most realistically and most practically speaking, to borrow the insights of historian of religion Jonathan Z. Smith, the cognitive power of the best translations lies in their incongruity, their surprise, in their *difference* from the original.[41] Partial, corrigible, never wholly adequate, translation is always a kind of "redescription," a re*inscription* of difference. Otherwise, we are back to the impossible transparencies of Borges's Menard, his comic though quietly terrifying book of mirrors, a total introjection of the other. Difference and even a certain incongruity in translation need hardly be betrayal (alone), but is, potentially—as an act of beholding that preserves the ongoing particularity of the original while creating something new in the receiving language, most loyal and, strangely perhaps, most loving. Meaning-content of the work translated can be enhanced by the very motion of linguistic transfer, however free or literal, and each (potential) return to the original is made richer by contact with other tongues in the charged fields of its translations. Dissemination in the acts of translation need not be dissimulation, an erosion of the power of the "original"; it can also imply a kind of generative *jouissance,* a multiplicity that increases pleasure. To quote Smith, in the broader context of intercultural translations, it may be true that *traduttori traditori,* but "in culture as in language, it is difference that generates meaning."[42]

Beyond Indologese

Issues of translation, particularly literary translation, are notoriously complex, particularly between languages as fundamentally different in syntax and prosody from English as Sanskrit, Tamil, and Prākrit. Formally there are many choices one has to make, from vocabulary, tone, word order, meter (if any), to line length and spacing. One has to constantly balance the sense of loyalty to the original text with the goal of producing a verse in English, something that will serve as more than a simple trot for the scholar-reader. I will simply quote one example to give these reflections practical grounding for readers of this book.[43] Veṅkaṭeśa has been particularly badly served by various forms of "Indologese," verse-forms dominated by Victorian vocabulary or indigestible prose summaries in archaic styles riddled with parentheses. The following is an example from a translation of *Devanāyakapañcāśat* (verse 40):

> O Devapati! Victory be to Your shanks which helped You in carrying messages (as the ambassador of Pāndavas), in carrying away the clothes of the cowherdesses and in following (hunting down) the asuras. They shine like (= are shaped like) Manmatha's bugles, quivers and vessels called Kalāchī.[44]

This is supposed to translate the following elegant, playful Sanskrit stanza, full of charm and a certain subtle power:

dūtye dukūlaharaṇe vrajasundarīṇām /
in being a messenger / in stealing the fine cloth *dukūla*
  dresses / of the lovely girls of Vraj
daityānudhāvana vidhau api labdhasāhyam //
pursuing the daityas / in being expedient / also/[they] helped
  you obtain
kandarpa-kāhala-niṣaṅga-kalācika-ābham /
of Kāma-viṇā / stringed instument or drum-quiver-waterpot-like /
  resembling
jaṅghāyugam jayati devapati tvadīyam //
pair of calves / victory! / O Lord of Gods / of you.

I have rendered this verse as follows, trying to hold to word order, and to a certain suspense—to the string of descriptive phrases in the original that leads, at the end, in a funneling motion, to the object of the verse: the calves of the deity/temple image:

When you ran as messenger
    between armies
or when you snatched the fine *dukūla* dresses
    from the pretty cowgirls
of Vraj—

        even when you ran down
the fleeing daityas,
they were there
to help you.
          They shine like the slender vīṇā, the drum,
the quiver,

        and golden waterpot
of Kāma,
  divine Lord of desire:
May your two fine calves be victorious!

Prosody and the Lines on the Page

As is obvious from the above example, though I try to hold in general to word order, and even in many cases, to the "left-branching" syntax of Sanskrit and Tamil poetry, I do not attempt to translate into English some version of the meter, rhyme pattern, or line length of the original. I have attempted to match, throughout these translations, the varying complex and densely configured semantic, syntactic, metric rhythms of the originals in the *visual* placement of words on the page, to mime the breath-lines—slow and loping, or swift, and clean—of Tamil, Sanskrit, or Prākrit meters by placement on the page. Though my translations have no fixed meter, they are certainly far from random or "free" in the loose sense of the term. I have thought long and hard on the spacing of English phrases, and it is the original that has guided me in my choices in English, even when the translation seems to differ most from the original *in form*. For instance, in the first verse of the Tamil *Navamaṇimālai*, Veṅkaṭeśa writes a clipped rhythmic, internally rhyming, alliterative and elliptical phrase *oru caṭai o<u>nr</u>iya kaṅkai tanta<u>n</u>a*—literally [the "Lord's flower feet"] that gave the Gaṅgā, [that was] mingled in a lock [of Śiva's matted hair]." In my English this becomes a line broken into visual rhythmic fragments:

they gave us the Gaṅgā
   who fell, caught
by a single lock
   of Śiva's
matted
      hair...

This being said, I often construct densely spaced English verse-lines to match, for instance, a tightly constructed wall of Veṅkaṭeśa's Tamil verses in the rich and complex *āciriyappā* meter. At other times, my English verse is lean, elegant, and simple, matching the more economical original Tamil *ve<u>n</u>pā* meter.[45] Veṅkaṭeśa's Tamil *Mumaṇikkōvai* and *Navamaṇimālai*, and his Sanskrit *Devanāyakapañcāśat* and *Gopālaviṃśati* are all in mixed meters, and the reader will notice that I vary the form of each verse on the page in English, variations that are meant to mirror the different syntactic and semantic registers in the original verses, their metrical densities or transparencies. As for the Prākrit *Acyutaśatakam*, it is composed in a single meter, the elegant, compact, often luminously simple *āryā* meter, and for this reason, though I use line breaks, indentations, and breath spacing on the page when appropriate to semantic content, the verse forms will seem more uniform and compact. In general, the thinness of my English verse-stanzas is meant here to reflect the leaner, more compact, simpler structure of the *āryā* meter.

Most commonly, the translations in this book take a middle path between literal fidelity to the originals on the page and adapting the meter (but not the meaning) of the originals—their own internal tensions, the slow or speeded up rhythm of consonants, long or short vowels, consonant clusters, line and syllable length—utilizing oral, audial, and visual conventions of contemporary American verse.[46]

Mumaṇikkōvai 4, for instance, more literally on the page, might look like this:

When the worlds are destroyed like bubbles that swell and burst
  in the rains
only you are not destroyed, O Lord true to your servants;
when we set ourselves to work testing what is true we find
  that you alone
are the truth of the precious Veda. O Devanāyaka, you
  dwell with Śrī,
your own divine splendor; you *are* the Śrī for she who adorns you;
your good nature shines like the moon with its light
a lovely well-oiled lamp of inextinguishable splendor;
you abide standing here a shoreless sea of nectar infinite
  accessibility joined with auspicious qualities like many jewels
  in the waters of the Milk Ocean;
you are a king who rules his subjects with grace choosing to ignore
  the faults of your servants; exalted Lord, you mingle with us
  here becoming for our sake
the Lord who lives in Ahīndra town; you have clothed yourself
  in all the *tattvas:*
the essential truths are the ornaments and weapons you wear on
  your great body
that glimmers like a dark multicolored gem;
you are the body of the most high vast Lord in the sky,
  inscrutable Vāsudeva;
you, his four *vyūhas,* transformations seen in deepest meditation:
assuming many other forms, the twelve names and the rest abiding,
your fine sweet forms are everywhere: Matsya the Fish the Tortiose
  the Boar

the Man-Lion and the Dwarf who measured the sky; the brahmin
with the axe
Paraśurāma the Sage and then two Rāmas the god-king and his brother;
as Kaṇṇaṉ of Dvāraka to ease Earth's burden,
and in time to come Kalki who will out of grace call an end to this
Kali Age.
After taking on many holy forms to destroy powerful karmas eager
to spread, you have come to this place so your good servants
might taste here the perfect sweetness of heaven. You along with
Śrī are the one life-breath of the world;
your bliss is to give life to all growing things;
you hide in all things, though no one knows the secret; pervading
every perfect and suitable body you yet surpass yourself, you stand
beyond it all
you fill us with wonder.
We do not see any other way or goal in this world but you alone
who accept our surrender. The pure Veda discerns infinite
means and forms of existence
all of which are your forms, you, abiding
the many means to the one goal.

Although this kind of placement of lines in English does potentially work in its own way, and would demand its own aesthetic conventions in English, the final form of the translation, forming breath-lines, and a certain visualization of pace and syntactic tension, mediates between various forces of new creation and mimesis across very different languages.

Only rarely do I add an extra English word or phrase to fill out the original. This would be to give the reader a sense of a rich image or set of images that are contained in a single Sanskrit, Tamil, or Prākrit word or phrase, or to fill out a too-elliptical phrase (as the one above about the god Śiva). Such a fill-in occurs in my translation of verse 49 of the Prākrit *Acyutaśatakam*. The phrase is *ghaṇakandalikandakaalīkhambhasamāim*: "resembling the [soft] stems of plantain (*kadalī*) and roots of thick *kandalī*." Both these images are mean to evoke frailty and transience—for some commentators *ghaṇa* also has the separate meaning of "cloud"—but *kandalikanda* houses a particularly evocative image. In Tamil, as the commentators note, white-flowering *kandalī* evokes *nāykkuṭai*, a small frail growth seen in fields after rain.

I have tried in my translation of this Prākrit verse to foreground this image, which has called for a bit of padding. I quote below the original verse, and my translation. Note also, following the discussion above, the economical *āryā* meter in the original, and, even with the addition of a phrase, the corresponding tightness of the English verse lines:

ṇa mahenti ṇaṇavantā taraṅgaḍiṇḍirabubbuasaricchāim /
do not take as great / those who know / of waves in the sea / foam /
bubbles / resembling
vihipamuhāṇa paāiṃ ghaṇakandalikandakaalīkhambhasamāim:
beginning with Brahmā and others / realms: stations / thick:
or clouds / *kandalī* roots / *kadalī* or plantain stems / resembling.

Those who know think little of the starry realms of Brahmā
and the others

those places like the bubbles and spume of waves or clouds
the soft stems of plantain

or the frail roots of white-flowering *kandalī*

thick in fields
after rain.

This Book and Its Tradition

I see this book ideally side by side with other translations of Indian literature that I have long admired, and that have provided for me various, sometimes opposed, models of translation. In the acknowledgments I have already spoken of the work of A. K. Ramanujan, and above, of Hank Heifetz; there is also the work of Martha Selby in Sanskrit, Prākrit, and Tamil; and that of David Shulman, Indira Peterson, and particularly of George Hart, whose commitment to an English style that better reflects the densely woven, compact syntactic and semantic structures of Tamil and Sanskrit in the original poems continues to challenge me to move closer to original line breaks and rhythm while preserving a contemporary free-verse form.[47] As any translator will admit, this is an ongoing process, and one that rather haunts the writer than consoles. As for older influences, the translations of Panikkar's *Mantramañjarī* and the still-compelling, more poetically idiosyncratic, versions of Sanskrit and Prākrit poems in Masson and Merwin's collection, *The Peacock's Egg*, first inspired me to want to study Sanskrit and Prākrit.[48] I read and savored the English translations of *Ṛg Veda* and the luminous poetry of the Upaniṣads, the Sanskrit love lyrics of Kālidāsa, Bhavabhūti, and the *Amaruśatakam*, and the Prākrit love poetry of Hāla's *Sattasāī*, all of which in turn invited me deeper into the poems and languages that were their sources.

It is my hope that the translations in this book will inspire readers not only who know something of Veṅkaṭeśa's languages and south Indian devotional tradition, but will inspire those who have not yet studied the three magnificent languages used here by one of the most remarkable poets of medieval south India.

2

A Necklace of Three Jewels for the Lord of Gods: The *Mummaṇikkōvai*

I

O Devanāyaka Lord of Gods you abide
as a giver of knowledge;
you have placed your truth and your very body
  at the feet
of those who serve you;[1]
your tender mercy[2] has taken the shape of a woman who
  shines sweetly for us,
a lamp that destroys our darkness;
she shines like a garland on your chest with its jewel,[3]
  on your holy body
    dark as a mountain
  of emerald.
        Gracefully she descends out of love along
          with you,[4]
becoming the female of whatever form you take;[5]
  hearing desperate prayers,
she cries them back to you, eager to help destroy
    our thick swarms
of karma.
        Your Lady Śrī who stands at your side,
her body joined inseparably to yours:
she gives mercy. Those who reach her feet
    touch you.

2

On the chest of Tirumāl
our Lord true to his servants

the eternal abode
of the big lovely
goddess

hang many strings of jewels—

and along with these jewels he has adorned himself
with my *Mummaṇikkōvai,*
this necklace of words.[6]

3

The heroine's girlfriend speaks:
Kāma the God of Love will shower a rain of flower-tipped arrows
from his charming sugarcane bow

at that young girl who longs for the soft feet
of the god of Truth:

mercy and grace [7]
gush from his sidelong glances.

He dwelt here a sea of sweet nectar,[8]
saying to those who longed
to plunge into him:
"Come, dive deep!"

He has come to Ahīndrapuram,
the town of the serpent king,
where those who speak
speak
the essence
of the three Vedas.

4

O Lord true to your servants only you are not destroyed
when the worlds are destroyed like bubbles that swell and burst
in the rains;
when we set ourselves to work
testing what is true,[9]

we find that you alone are the truth of the precious Veda.
O Devanāyaka you dwell with Śrī, your own divine splendor;
you *are* the Śrī
   for she who adorns you.[10]
Your good nature shines like the moon with its light,
a lovely well-oiled lamp
   of inextinguishable
         splendor.
                                        You abide,
standing here a shoreless sea of nectar,[11]
   infinite accessibility joined with auspicious qualities[12]
like many jewels in the waters of the Milk Ocean.
You are a king who rules his subjects with grace[13]
choosing to ignore the faults of your servants;
exalted Lord you mingle with us here,
         becoming, for our sake
the Lord who lives in Ahīndra town.
You have clothed yourself in all the *tattvas:*
   the essential truths[14] are the ornaments and weapons you wear
            on your great body
that glimmers like a dark
   multicolored gem.[15]
You are the body of the most high, vast Lord in the sky,
   inscrutable Vāsudeva; you, his four *vyūhas,*
transformations seen in deepest
   meditation:[16]
assuming many other forms, the twelve names and the
   rest, abiding,
      your fine sweet forms
   are everywhere:[17]
Matsya the Fish[18] the Tortoise the Boar the Man-Lion
   and the Dwarf who measured the sky;
the brahman with the axe Paraśurāma the Sage
   and then two Rāmas the god-king and his brother;
as Kaṇṇaṉ of Dvāraka to ease Earth's burden, and in time
   to come
Kalki who will out of grace call an end
      to this Kali Age.
After taking on many holy forms to destroy powerful karmas
   eager to spread,

you have come to this place so your good servants might
taste here
the perfect sweetness
of heaven.[19]
You along with Śrī are the one life-breath
of the world;
your bliss is to give life to all growing things;[20]
you hide in all things, though no one knows the secret; pervading
every perfect and suitable body
you yet surpass
yourself,
you stand beyond it all,
you fill us with wonder.[21]
We do not see any other way or goal in this world but
you alone[22]
who accept our surrender.
The pure Veda discerns infinite means and forms of existence,
all of which are your forms,
you, abiding,
the many means to the one goal.[23]

5

Filled with perfect knowledge
that gives unshakable confidence
in the essence
of the pure Veda

we have become the slaves
of Nārāyaṇa alone—

he who lives in the town of the serpent king
where Vedas
are chanted by their keeper
Lotus-Born
Brahmā.

6

The concerned friend speaks, seeing the condition of the heroine:
Sighing, she sees the black cloud come to rest
over Medicine Hill
in the town of the serpent king:

streams of sweet mercy rain
on its people.

Quivering with desire
shrinking from shame

wet with sweat
hair standing on end,
her eyes fill

with tears.

A wild peacock of the hills
screaming its desire
in love:

What shall we say when they see her?

7

When knowledge is given you are the known;
when light shines you are illumination;
when we delight in the coolness of shelter you are mother;
when you stand before creation you are father;
if in misfortune we are not abandoned you are our kin;
when we give up passions and pleasure you are the fruit;
when we are graced with a path you are the way;[24]
when wickedness is crushed you are the embodiment
of Dharma;[25]
when we are alone you are our friend;
when the fair Lady sits on your chest you are pure;
when you are Nārāyaṇa you are the world's cause;
when we attain a high place in heaven you are the
wish-giving tree;
in the absence of even one defect you are the supreme Lord of all;
when our grief is broken
you are sweet bliss;[26]
when you are within me
then you *are* me;
when there is nothing except you,
I am yours;[27]
when Evil vanishes you are Good;
when the universe that was swallowed is spat out again

you become power.
O true Lord
even the Vedas know nothing to equal
the quintessence
of your being.

8

Meru, the golden mountain
became the perfect waterpot to wash the foot
of Nārāyaṇa

raised that very day

from this very place

to highest
heaven:

our dark god the color of the sea
the cause of all things

stood here:

descending, be came to Tiruvahīndrapuram,
the town of the serpent king,
he who is desired
even by
the Vedas.

9

The foster mother speaks to her mother:
We are utterly confused by our girl slender as a creeper
her long eyebrows
curved like bows,

the very image of god's Red Lady
sitting in the Lotus.

She stands there hungry for mercy; she hears with wonder
of his dwelling
in the town of the serpent king—

our god
the only cure for the sickness of bad karma
one with the holy hill.

10

Unbegotten, you are the father of all things:
those who resort to proper means obtain you,
  without you
they cannot secure happiness;[28]
you don't exist for my sake but for your sake alone:
the many forms of the world appear like lightning
from your dark icon.[29]
          Those who reach your feet
become your equals,
    but without your tender love[30]
they do not even
  draw a breath.[31]
        O first cause!
Primal Father
  who came
    at the Elephant's
    first cry.

Afterword

We begin this anthology with the first of two of Veṅkaṭeśa's surviving Tamil poems for Devanāyaka, mentioned in the account of his vision of the Lord near the river Peṇṇai: his *Mummaṇikkōvai.*

Mummaṇikkōvai (A *Kōvai* of Three Jewels) refers to a Tamil genre of love poetry used by many saint-poets; it is one of ninety-six kinds of *prabandhams* in classical Tamil. As Norman Cutler has noted, the *kōvai* is an outgrowth of classical Tamil *akam* ("interior" or love) poetry, and shares many of its conventions, along with a characteristic bhakti mingling of *puṟam* ("exterior," war/heroic/royal/historic) themes.[32] It is technically defined as a love poem (*kōvai*) that includes ten verses in three different meters (the *akaval* [*āciriyappā*], *veṉpa*, and *kalitturai*) that are connected by *antāti*, that is, in each case the last word of one verse is the first word of the next, and so forth. Veṅkaṭeśa's poem, being ten verses long, is, for unknown reasons, incomplete.[33]

We are made aware right away in the *Mumaṇikkōvai* of Veṅkaṭeśa's earlier Āḻvār Tamil models. In the very first pada of the first verse the epithet for Devanāyaka in Tamil—*aṭiyarpāṉ meyyai*—The Lord of Truth [or of Body] for His Servants—is taken from Tirumaṅkaiyāḻvār's *tirumoḻi* of this same form of Vishnu, translated in the last section of this anthology. In the usual form of the epithet, *aṭiyavārkku meyyanē, mey* can mean "truth" or "body," emphasizing this Lord of Truth as one who places his body at the feet of those who surrender to Him—his servants or "slaves" (*aṭi*). The Āḻvār reference here could not be clearer, while the significance of Devanāyaka as the Lord "of *mey*"—a god who offers not only his "truth" but also his very "body" to his servants—will become more and more clear as we read both Tamil poems to this vividly embodied Vishnu of Tiruvahīndrapuram.

The *prabandham* begins with an evocation to Śrī/Lakṣmī, "Tiru" in Tamil, "luminous adornment," and the goddess consort of Vishnu; in Sanskrit the Śrī of "Śrīvaiṣṇava," the feminine power (*śakti*) and mercy (*aruḷ*) of the male Vishnu; "the female of whatever form" the god takes. Vishnu and Śrī are, together, the single Godhead of Śrivaiṣṇavas; in the language of the poem, "those who reach [her] feet also touch Him."[34] From here, after a verse describing the poem as a "necklace" of words to place on the bejeweled body of god (verse 2),[35] and an *akam* love lyric about divine longing in the voice of a girlfriend (*tōḻi*) of the heroine (*talaivi*), the poem oscillates between the poles of divine majesty and intimacy. Devanāyaka is awesome in power, a king of creation (*aracaṉ*) who has taken many cosmic, natural, and human forms—from fierce Paraśurāma and the Man-Lion, to sweet Krishna and heroic Rāma—in every cosmic age to sustain and "save" the worlds from darkness and evil karma (see verses 4, 7, 8, 10). He is the "essence (*poruḷ*) of precious Veda," the Lord who "stands" a "shoreless sea of nectar" (an image that evokes both containment and flow, a flowing channeled upward), the single "life-breath" (*uyir*) of the world; but he is also our most precious, personal Beloved, who "mingles" his own self (*kalantaṉai*) with us "here" on earth, in the sacred ground of the temple, makes love to us, and leaves us (verses 3, 4, 6, 9). We tremble in his presence, our hair stands on end, we sweat and sigh, our body liquefies in love (*aṉpu*); we become open and vulnerable, crying "our desire in love," like the young girl who goes into ecstasies as the Lord appears as the monsoon cloud over the temple hill (verse 6, which uses all the classical Tamil *akam* conventions of love and the personae—mother, foster-mother, young girl—of the love poem). This verse 6, and verse 9 about the "confusion" (*mayakkam*) of the foster-mother over the sickness of the heroine caused by separation from her Beloved, remain some of the most striking examples of post-Āḻvār uses of classical Tamil poetic forms in the context of religious devotion. This is love at its most disruptive and troublesome.

The *Mumaṇikkōvai* elegantly draws together various polarities in the heart of the godhead, fusing together in one theological and personal vision Vishnu as Pure Being, united with "his Tiru," the Divine as Other, primordial splendor, "inscrutable Vāsudeva," Father, and Power (verse 4), as the tutelary god of "this place" who "stood" (*niṉṟa*, verse 8), with the personal god whom we love and who loves us (all too briefly) in return, then withdraws: a god both of absence and sweet magisterial presence.

Over and over again, as we come to a most intimate experience of beholding and being beheld, and held, touched, we are also made aware of distance, the asymmetry of lover-beloved. These are the key willed ambiguities of love in Veṅkaṭeśa's poetics. Distance and intimate encounter: this oscillation, this rhythm of desire, is at the heart of the poems, and at the heart of religious love in Veṅkaṭeśa's theology. All seems out of our control, even our sudden awareness of deep indissoluble union. Ultimately, in Veṅkaṭeśa's devotional poetics, beyond our willing it, in various discrete and particular encounters, we are suddenly made aware that Vishnu/Devanāyaka is "our" god; "my" god; He is within me; He is mercy and grace (*aruḷ*), love (*aṉpu*) and "sweetness" (*iṉpam*), within "you" and within the very structures of intimate address itself. Verse 7, in a funneling or telescoping motion common to all of Veṅkaṭeśa's praise-poems in this book, traces this fusion of opposing identities: after a litany of praises that index Vishnu/Devanāyaka's cosmic immanence, the poet levels his gaze into the very heart of the human person:

when our grief is broken
  you are sweet bliss;
When you are within me,
  then you *are* me;
when there is nothing except you,
  I am yours!

The *Mummaṇikkōvai* "ends" with an image of radical mercy (*aruḷ*) and divine tender love (*aṉpu*): the rescue of the distressed elephant king devotee Gajendra from the jaws of a crocodile, one of the most popular stories in south Indian bhakti.[36] In spite of its fragmentary status, this *prabandham* is remarkably comprehensive in thematic structure. The Lord responds to Gajendra's cry for help, and one imagines Veṅkaṭeśa believing in the power of his own prayer of surrender (*prapatti*) beyond will, beyond hope.[37]

3

A Garland of Nine Jewels: The *Navamaṇimālai*

I

They ravished the hearts of those lovers who know no
other beloved;
stretching out to contain them,
they measured the worlds;
they gave us the Gaṅgā,
who fell, caught
by a single lock
of Śiva's
matted
hair;
they made into a dance stage
the serpent's broad hoods;
they stood firm in this very place as the most exalted
means of salvation and ran, on the field of battle,
to deliver
the message of Dharma;
they conquered chaos, crushing demon Śakaṭa
into fine powder—
they are called sweet medicine
drunk by the slaves
of the Lord;
joined without seam

to the red hands of Lady Śrī, they exude the fragrance of fresh
shining *tulasī*,
and glitter with anklets filled with precious gems.
They kicked a girl out of stone that day long ago;
of rare eminence, they stand
at the end
of the Vedas,
and raised up,
they touch
even the top
of Brahmā's
head!
They came to live here, in Tiruvahīndrapuram
to give grace and mercy:
the flower feet
of the Lord
who is true to his servants.

2

You churned havoc in the ocean's depths when you kept
on growing
in your body of the Fish;
as the Tortoise you bore Mt. Mandara as the churning stick
on your back; you redeemed Vasudhā the earth when you
broke open the chest
of that demon, Hiraṇyākṣa;
you leapt from the pillar as an act of truth
for the boy, splitting into two the body of powerful Hiraṇyakaśipu;
and just as you promised,
you gave back the three worlds
to your own *devatās*, after spanning them
with your foot.
As Paraśurāma you hacked your enemies into little pieces;
as Rāma you cut off the ten heads of ten-headed Rāvaṇa,
the king who refused you honor;
as Bālarāma you destroyed Pralambāsura
when he came in fitting disguise as a small calf
in Gokula; as Krishna, out of love for Tuvarai[1] you lifted the entire
mountain
with one bare left hand,

and on a proud agile horse,
you will yet come again to earth
to obliterate suffering.
Here you have become a good and pleasant
hill of medicine
that heals the sickness of bad karma;[2]
you take delight in the swift flood waters
of the Garuḍa River flowing
at your holy feet.
You who taught the husband of the Lady of the Tongue
the Vedas' first syllable *a*, who honored Garuḍa, the son of Viṇatā,
with new life,
when he surrendered to you.
You who give to Ananta, your snake,
the joy to worship your feet,
letting him coil himself into a couch for those
holy feet.
O Devanāyaka, Lord of truth to your servants,
you have come to Tiruvahīndrapuram,
this place
born from the womb of Bhūdevī,
goddess of earth!

3

He is a trickster who taught false doctrine
to those demons who took the shape
of flying cities;

his body dark as a rain cloud,
he stopped
the rain,

lifting a mountain
with one
upraised arm;[3]

his hands bent back the bow whose arrows
would suck dry
the wave-tossed sea:

He is the Lord of Truth to his servants,
giving mercy and grace,

he destroys
our karmas.[4]

4

Devanāyaka of matchless radiance,
married to the great Lotus Lady
of fragrant
hair—

he comes in delight to cool groves in the sand,[5]

after bathing in the sea
in the month of Māci—

this great virile God of Love
riding his Bird!

5

O Lord who kicked the demon Śakaṭa
when she rolled herself into a ball;
who swallowed, spat out
and spanned
with your foot,
the seven worlds:

I count as affliction passions
that burn like fire
and delights of worldly riches.[6]
I have returned
to your service.

O Lord true to your servants, take up in your hands,
at the time of my death,
when ignorance
and confusion overwhelm me,
Your radiant Conch
and Discus!
Gracefully come to me,
grant to me your knowledge

and your sweet
mercy!

6

You stood here O Lord who long ago became the simple cowherd boy
and king, the Protector
who eased Earth's burden when you killed King Kaṃsa,
dreaded by gods, and the mad elephant, the wrestlers,
swift proud Śakaṭam
and deceitful Pūtanā.
O Lord of Truth to your servants,
your lovely body is dark as lamp-black
as the deep blue
kāyā blossom.[7]
O munificent king who showers grace like torrents from a monsoon cloud
over Ayintai town,
if we do not forget the beauty of your body,
we will not be born
again![8]

7

Your holy body is dark as the blue *neytal* lily;
as sapphire, a great
rain cloud; a peacock's neck,
the wide sea,
kohl for the eyes.[9]
I took refuge in you. I became the slave
of the Lord of celestials,
Lord, body of Truth
to his servants—[10]
You protected the Elephant,
Discus in your hand! You live in the great town
of the king of serpents!
O god, have mercy on me!
Say: "Do not fear!"
Come to me, on the day of my death,
so the servants of Yama, God of the Dead,
do not drag
me away!

8

O Lord of inexhaustible beauty who dwells in Ayintai town,
rich in groves that catch

the passing clouds
in their tops,[11]
flawless Vāsudeva[12] who protected the cows of Vraj
when you lifted the mountain.
Bearer of prosperity and brightest effulgence,
O Devanāyaka,
driving the chariot, you became a faultless messenger
who served the will of his beloved Pāṇḍavas,
warriors whose words
are true.[13]
Invincible Acyuta[14] who destroys the sins of those who serve you,
O Lord of Gods true to your servants,
before I stumble
and fall
faint,
overwhelmed and weak,
pulled down
as the noose thrown around my neck by Yama's messengers
tightens,
and, as I hear
their lisping obscenities,
you say: "Do not fear!
Do not fear!
Do not fear!"
wanting only
to protect me.

9

My arrogance mixed with passion, this fire,[15]
takes root, and spreads, heaping
contrary knowledge
upon ignorance
joined to my own many
faults:

when these vanish,
each in their own proper way,[16]
what else need I desire?

O Devanāyaka, I have no peace of mind:
graciously accept my resolute surrender[17]

by your mercy and grace[18]
that will not see me
suffer!

10

After praising him with fifty verses in the ancient tongue,[19]
singing a hundred songs in charming Prākrit,[20]
and stringing a three-jeweled necklace
of songs, my *Mummaṇikkōvai*, in the graceful Tamil tongue,[21]
I sung these songs: a *pantu* a *kalal* an *ammāṉai* a *ūcal* an *ecal*[22]
and the praiseworthy *Navamaṇimalai*
at the two feet
of the Lord
of ever-prosperous serpent town.

These are the fruits of Mukunda's mercy,
when he said to me:
"Sing in your own words what is sung
in the old Veda!"[23]

Afterword

This Tamil poem shares many themes with the *Mumaṇikkōvai*. There are motifs that allude to classical Tamil and the Tamil of the Āḻvār saint-poets—here, most markedly, in a reference in verse 4 to bathing with the icon in the month of Māci, near "cool casuarina groves in the sand" (*maṇal tōppil*). This evokes not only images from old Tamil fertility rituals performed by girls during the months of Tai and Māci in the hopes of obtaining good husbands, rituals that blend sensuality and fertility, but Āḻvār Āṇṭāḷ's adaptation of this old ritual to describe "bathing" with Vishnu, as a lover and husband, combining in her own way the erotic with the nuptial.[24] But even more vividly than in the *Mummaṇikkōvai*, the *Navamaṇimālai*, in a telescoping fashion, traces the various forms of Vishnu at Tiruvahīndrapuram, from the transcendental worlds of heaven, the "flower-feet" that spanned the compass points in verse 1, mythic images of supernal power, the god who crushed demons, who took on ten forms (the *daśāvatāras* of verse 2) to conquer various demons in various ages, the god of the old stories who creates, sustains, and destroys worlds, the Vishnu of the battlefield of Kurukṣetra in the *Bhagavad Gītā*, to the god who "dwelled" here (*niṉṟa*, past participle) and still dwells here, in the shrine landscape, as the Medicine Hill at Tiruvahīndrapuram, the beautiful body of the icon in the shrine's sanctum, and finally, most minutely, the god "dwelling/abiding/standing," (*ni<u>n</u><u>r</u>a*, as an icon "stands") in the depths of a devotee's heart.[25]

Throughout the poem the poet, like the Ā<u>l</u>vārs before him, delights in seeing the Big in the Little, all of the cosmos, its harrowing fascinating majesty, contained in the stone or bronze feet of a temple icon, or in the imagined body of Krishna, the child-god, the "simple cowherd boy" (verse 6) who "eased Earth's burden" when he killed King Kaṃsa and numerous demons, from wrestlers and mad elephants, to the demoness Pūtanā. The *Navamaṇimālai* is dominated by images and allusions to Krishna (see verses 1, 2, 5, 6, 8), a form of Vishnu that lends itself well to this theme of the Big in the Little, majesty and power fully present in the humanlike, accessible body of a child, a young man, hero and friend to the "beloved Pāṇḍavas" (verse 8).[26] This accessible, lovable Krishna form of Vishnu/Devanāyaka will reach an apotheosis in Veṅkaṭeśa's *Gopālaviṃśati*, a poem in praise of the "Cowherd God" also written for Devanāyaka Swāmi at Tiruvahīndrapuram, translated below.

This allusion to Krishna's lovely, powerful bodies brings to the fore one of the most important themes of this poem, and of Veṅkaṭeśa's bhakti poetics as a whole: the at once aesthetic and religious focus on the beautiful body of god. Verses 6 and 7 not only index the concrete ritual presence of a god in a consecrated icon or evoke a vivid word-picture of the god of past sacred narratives, remembered with the creative powers of a poet's imagination but also refer to a deity who lives and plays, both physically and supernaturally, before us, as would a human beloved. But this is no normal beloved, and no normal body. It is a perfected form, somehow contained in the material temple image. The body of Vishnu in Veṅkaṭeśa's devotional poetics is physical, actual, while remaining transcendental, a figure of awesome power. Above all, this body is "beautiful," blue-black as *añca<u>n</u>am* (lamp-black) or the deep blue *kāyā* blossom. Veṅkaṭeśa's god is a *super*-aesthetic god; a god who appears as "beauty" itself (*a<u>l</u>aku*), a purified, impassible beauty *that saves.* As Veṅkaṭeśa says in verse 6 of the *Navamaṇimālai*, those "who do not forget" the "beauty" of that body "will not be born again."[27]

Before ending with a verse that perhaps first inspired the story of Veṅkaṭeśa's encounter with Lord Devanāyaka on the road to Kāñcīpuram, and his systematic composition of praises for Devanāyaka in all three of his working languages, his "Veda" couched in "his own words" (*va<u>l</u>i mo<u>l</u>i*), we have in verse 9 a formal, ritual surrender (*ataikkalam*) to the Lord. Though the poet seems to lay claim to helplessness here, and is witness to a lack that can never be resolved, love's wound that can never be healed, his passionate appeal to grace/mercy/power-potential of "presence" (*aruḷ*) is itself an act of will (self-effort) that is thought to draw the attention of Vishnu, who now has a suitable "pretext" (*vyāja*) to save the poet from worldly passions that burn us like fire (*poruḷum aḻalum*).[28]

In this way the poem inscribes two seemingly antithetical truths at the heart of Veṅkaṭeśa's theology of devotion: divine-human asymmetry and the intimacy of particular love.

4

Fifty Verses for the Lord of Gods: The *Devanāyakapañcāśat*

1

His lotus feet are drenched by sticky nectar dropped by garlands of *mandāra*[1] blossoms
that circle the tall crowns of gods
who prostrate before him;[2]

worshiped by Śiva, Lord of Beasts,
and Brahmā,
the creator,

he is Lord of the town of the serpent king,
his eyes long and broad
as lotus petals—

may Devanātha, the Lord of Gods,
protect me.

2

I bow down to the long line of our teachers, protectors of worlds:
in the beginning,[3] Devanātha, the Lord;
Kamalā, His consort;
and Pṛtaneśa, commander of heaven.[4]
In the shining center, Nātha and Vakulabhūṣaṇa,[5]
and adorning the crown, Rāmānuja
and the others.

3

They point out to us those sacred fords
along the shores of the Lord of Gods' holy sea of mercy,[6]
a refuge for the three worlds:
again and again
I do homage to those ancient poets[7]

beginning with Vālmīkī[8]
whose words speak truth, sweet to the ear,
like the Veda.[9]

4

O mother who dwells in the Lotus[10]
I make of you this small
humble request—
grant me this favor:[11]

that this Lord of Gods, your beloved, might listen to my words
as you would the prodigious
prattling

of a little
child.[12]

5

O Lord of Gods
surely I am gifted enough to praise you whose glory
is discerned by the Veda's
most exalted revelation:[13]

would the herds of mother cows
who drink the sweet waters of the Milk Ocean
let their calves
feed
on grass?

6

Those such as Ananta and Garuḍa
cannot fathom the full extent of your being;[14]

even those steeped
in yogic trance[15]

can see only a small
fragment
of your glory:[16]

I long to praise you,
you who grant us our heart's deepest desires—
come, earn that title of yours:

"Lord of Truth
to His Servants."[17]

7

O Primal Lord of the serpent king,
bestowing upon me a tongue of deep and fertile powers,[18]
untouched
by the censure of learned
connoisseurs,[19]

let your name, chanted by Vyāsa,
most austere
of sages,
bear fruit:

be *fit for*, be *fond of*, praise;

be the praise
and the
praiser himself![20]

8

Even though I've long wandered so far from you,
with the burden of my heavy bonds
hard to untangle,[21]

I look to you alone for protection, O Lord of Gods.

And oh so steadily,
of your own accord,
out of innate compassion,

you draw me
to yourself
like a bird
on a string![22]

9

My mind, duped by the myriad mirages of pleasures
and passion
now finds solace in you,
only Lord of Gods:
It enters you, cool sweet god,
as into a cool, sweet and brimming
pool of deep water
in the heat
of summer.[23]

10

O Lord of Gods, they say your radiant forms[24]
are eternal
in the heavenly realm;
on the Ocean of Milk
and on the highest limb
of Veda;
at the very center of the Sun's circle,[25]
in good people's
hearts,[26]
and here,
on Brahmācalam[27]
the holy hill
revered by sages.

11

O Lord, gods bow down to Auṣadhagiri
Medicine Herb Hill, girt by holy shrines
that destroy evil and misfortune,[28]
beloved by the serpent Śeṣa, by Bhūdevī, goddess Earth,
by Garuḍa and by Viriñca,
our Brahmā:
this hill, made famous[29] by you
who are good medicine for those who fall
at your feet.

12

O Bhagavān,[30]
   though the majesty and power of the entire universe
bends to your will,[31]

those who know origins and ends,
what is above
   and what is below,
like to call you[32]
   Devanāyaka, "Lord of Gods."

It seems to me that perhaps by this[33]
they mean to show how your servants—

whose minds
   are adorned by devotion to you—
become gods
   in this place.

13

O Lord of the town of the serpent king,[34]
   the *tattvas*,
truths luminous and obscure,[35]
   enumerated by wise elders steeped
   in the three Vedas' supreme
revelation,[36]
   divided into
sentient and insentient forms:[37]

they shine
in this icon of yours[38]
as glittering weapons
   and jewels.

14

Seeing your lovely body whose splendor is made even
   more perfect
by each perfect
   limb,[39]

enjoyed by your beloved wives with unblinking, astonished
   eyes,[40] and sought out

by the jewels and weapons that adorn it
to increase their own radiance,

my sight, O Lord of Gods,
is not sated with
seeing!

15

O Lord of immortals,[41] the best of your hymns,
most esteemed by sages such as Vyāsa
and the others,
whose words are taught
by every other Veda,[42]
teaches this,

O all-pervading god:[43]

these lovely limbs of yours give birth to this entire
world of forms,[44]
beginning
with Brahmā!

16

O Lord,
even the crown[45] you wear on your head
shines with the combined light of a thousand suns,[46]
destroying
the deep dark night of my mind:

this indeed is fit proof
of your lordship
over gods.

17

O Lord of Gods,
a night smeared with stars,[47] the shining waves
of your dark curly locks of hair[48]
join with the moon of your face that drips bright nectar
of a tender smile:
this is fit object for our meditations[49]
to cool the burning fevers of births
and deaths.

18

With lips red as *bimbā* fruit, eyes like the full-blown lotus blossom
and dangling locks of dark hair,
your lovely face, made even more lovely by shining earrings
and, on the upper ear, the *karṇapūram*
like the golden long-
petaled
ketaka flower:[50]
your face,
O Lord of Gods,
adorns my mind.

19

That rare mark of auspicious grace—[51]
half-dark,
half-bright,
worn by the moon
for only a certain phase of it waxing,[52]

shines always on your brow

where, long ago, O Lord of Gods,
from the mere drop
of a drop
of sweat,[53]

was born
three-eyed Puruṣa, Lord Śiva
who wields
the spear.

20

Bearing the yellow mark of our teachers[54] on your sloping brow
like a strange streak of lightning from a shining monsoon cloud
raining beauty—[55]

O Lord of Gods,

it seems to me you have become an auspicious lamp
for a world
swallowed by darkness!

21

Those wise in the Veda, O Lord of Gods,
say your ears[56] are the source
of the four
wide directions;[57]

thus it is no wonder that these ears themselves,
hearing all creatures' cries of pain,
compel you
to answer their every
desire.[58]

22

On your lovely ear, O Lord of Gods, that shines
in flowing waves of beauty,
it takes the form of the Fish
that marks the banner of the love god,
enflamer of desires:[59]

Makarikā, this jeweled earring,
sweet to behold by those who stand before you,
plays frisky
games,[60]

swimming
against
your current.[61]

23

O Lord of Gods, Brahmā who sits in the Lotus
must look to your two eyebrows for guidance
in his royal duties of creation:[62]

if not,
then where in the world might he have found the original model
for the love god's great sugarcane bow
whose arrows strike all creatures
dumb with love?[63]

24

Its sweetness and goodness there to see and to touch;[64]
the fierce waves of its mercy flood its shores,

granting to all who plead
their every desire;
long, bright, and sleek,[65]
O Lord of Gods,
your eye is the double
of the wide shining
Milky Ocean.[66]

25

O Lord of those who ride the aerial cars,[67]
they are eager to play at the protection of the world,
miming the simple charms
of the lotus flower;[68]

sending streams of blissful perfumes,

they call to us, breathless,
with no words,
as from the quiet
of a mother's womb:[69]

the glances
from the reddened corners of your eye

drench me

with sweetest nectar.

26

O Lord of those who fly in space,[70]

your nose,
a bridge over the ocean of your eye,

snorts Vedas endlessly
from its nostrils,[71]

its sweet breath doubling
the fragrance
of your most beloved lady's lotus face:

and just now,
flooded by its coolness,

I am fanned awake
from my
swoon.[72]

27

O Lord of immortals, mad with love,[73]
my mind kisses your lower lip red as *bimbā* fruit,
as the tender young shoots
from the coral tree
of paradise:[74]

your lips enjoyed by young cowherd girls,
by your flute

and by the prince
of conch shells.

28

O Lord of Gods, like your long garland,
Vanamālikā, stirred into bright bloom,
my mind,
radiant with wonder[75]

becomes an ornament
for your neck
that wears fine tattoos
from Padmāvatī's lovely bangles[76]
like a conch
blue-black as the eye of a peacock's tail

from the glow of your
dark light.[77]

29

My mind,[78] giddy with love,[79] is held tight
in close embrace
by your long arms

circled by bracelets
that bristle
with many-colored jewels.

O chief of celestials,[80]

they hang down
to your knees,
ornaments for the weapons they hold,[81]

shining with scars
from the warrior's bowstring,

they win the war of boons
with Pārijāta, the coral tree
of paradise.[82]

30

Your Conch and Discus, O Lord of Gods, draw only silence
from your enemies;
rising like the Moon and Sun
in a single instant
over the dark blue sapphire hill of your body,[83]

they inspire, by their self-mastery and power[84]
the confidence of the world

in your right hand which grants fearlessness
to those
who love you.[85]

31

Like red coral in the depths of the still sea of your mercy,
beauty and bliss to your lovers,[86] O Lord of Gods,

your right hand unfurls like a lotus,
bestows the gesture "do not fear":

it shines in my heart that shakes with terrors
of endless sins.[87]

32

O Lord of Gods, enjoying, between your two arms,
your hero's chest[88]
daubed
with auspicious designs,[89]
curvy half-moon

scars
    from the darts of vicious
runaway
  demons[90]

and marked with the mole and its curl of white hair, Śrīvatsa,

  with Kaustubhā,
  Queen Gem of the Milky Sea,

with Lady Ramā
  and the long garland
    Vanamālikā—[91]

the arrow of our thought
  has hit
    its mark.

33

In its ordered array of attributes,[92]
  in the extravagant profusion of its many colors,[93]
the lovely smile of its fresh-blown flowers—[94]
  close to the heart
  and sweet of fragrance,
cleaving to Kamalā and the Queen of Gems,[95]
  and, O Lord of Gods,
  eternal—

this Vanamālikā,
  shines
    like a twin
of your icon.[96]

34

Cool and moist, pure luminous destroyer of darkness,
bright asylum for stars;[97]

dripping sweet
  nectar for gods,[98]
desire's passionate
  yes:[99]

O Lord of Gods,

such a wonderous thing is this mind of yours,[100]

that gives birth to moons
in every
creation!

35

Though it is so thin,
O Lord of gods,
it swallowed

and spat out

this entire
universe;

its three soft
folds
mark nothing less

than the threefold
division
of worlds;[101]

in its fragrant lotus navel
a bee
the shape of Viriñca,
Lord Brahmā,
has its little house:[102]

like a waistband

my mind

adorns
your sweet belly.

36

The pollen dust from your lotus navel
is the stuff of gods;
its many transformations obtain first rank among the dwellers
of heaven.

And because these gods, in ordered array, bow down
to worship you

here, in this
place,[103]
how fitting is your epithet,

O Hero!
so worthy of praise,
Vibudhanāyaka,
"Lord of Celestials."

37

O Lord of Gods, the belt,
so finely wrought,

a dazzling well-born young girl
who circles your waist,[104]

enslaves my eyes:

wrapped in the yellow cloth,[105]
it thrills at the touch
of your left hand, resting on your thigh—

bristling with lovely beams of light

its hairs stand
on end.

38

They brought to birth a jewel among girls[106]
and bore the fertile third class of men;

a hero's death-bed for demon chieftains
and soft pillows for beloved consorts;

lovely as the long sinuous trunk
of a young elephant king,[107]

your twin thighs, O Lord of Gods,

draw my mind
deep.[108]

39

They are like surging whirlpools of light
that quiver
and play

in a floodtide
of beauty[109]

or beloved companions
of Lakṣmī's jeweled palace
mirrors;

yet they scuffed and crawled
their way
through crude cowherder's
courtyards:[110]

these two knees of yours
will not let go
of my mind.

40

When you ran as messenger
between armies
or when you snatched the fine *dukūla* dresses
from the pretty cowgirls
of Vraj—[111]

even when you ran down
the fleeing *daityas*,[112]

they were there
to help you.
They shine like the slender *vīṇā*, the drum,
the quiver,
and golden waterpot
of Kāma,
divine Lord of desire:[113]
May your two fine calves be victorious.

41

With its touch the young wife of the forest sage
emerged out of a stone;
ashes from a womb
became the handsome
young prince;

caressed by Lady Ramā
and Mahī,
goddess Earth,
they say

this foot
is the One God
of all.[114]

42

Even this heart of mine—
madly tossed
here
and there
by force of its desire
for every
other thing—[115]

clings to
and of its own accord
is held
captive,
O Lord of Gods,

by your toes:

flowing
downward

in the liquid light
of their own
rays,[116]

they are petals
of your divine
lotus feet.[117]

43

Their great waves of light wash clean my dirty water,
turning the Garuḍa River
into another Gaṅgā;
worshiped by rows of jeweled tiaras on the bowed heads
of celestials:

O Lord,

your toenails—
this twin row of shining jewels
on your holy feet.[118]

44

The long club the flag the goad the waterpot of sweet nectar;
a royal parasol the wish-
granting Kalpaka tree;
lotus and flowered gateway, Conch
and Discus, the sign
of the Fish, and of the other nine,[119]
O Lord of Gods,
may your honored foot
which bears these marks
become an ornament
for our
heads.

45

My god what a wonder:
the black letters of fate drawn into every crease
of our foreheads
by Brahmā himself,[120]

O Lord of Gods,

are blown away

at one and the same time,

beyond all yoga,[121]

by a touch
of the dust
from your lotus feet.[122]

46

For those who possess purity in duty and rites—[123]
something won after innumerable deaths and rebirths—
devotion to your feet

is sweetest joy.

O Lord of Gods,
but have you not said yourself
that those who have You
as their very life

and breath[124]

are rare indeed, hard to find:[125]

they are, in fact,

your very Self, the core
of Your being.[126]

47

But, O Lord of Gods, he who places the burden
of his own protection at your lotus feet—

his wealth
is his utter poverty;[127]

those worthies who have mastered all manner of yogas
made famous with many
many praises[128]
are not equal
to even a hundred-millionth
part
of such a one
as that.[129]

48

I was once the most refined thief of my own body
and soul;[130]

but now

O Lord of Gods,

I return to you what is your own,
something utterly useless to anyone else—[131]

take me back
to your feet

accept this self
as you would an anklet returned by the thief
   who stole it:
                  Only you
are fit to wear it.

49

Finding me—
an ocean of ignorance, chief beast among
the sinners, breaker of all rules
   the emperor of worthless fools—[132]

how can you,
        O Lord of Gods,
   who knows all things,

conceive of a better vessel
   for your
      mercy?

50

When such terrible disasters befell the boy Prahlāda, the
   cows of Gokula,
Gajendra, King of Elephants, Parīkṣit,
   and so many others,
didn't you protect them?

Well, all that's on one side; on the other,
      my own protection.

O Lord of Gods,
   weigh one against the other:

   which is heavier?

51

O supreme king of celestials,[133]
   my mind is turning
and turning
      in a whirling gyre
of pleasures
   and passion

with the force
of a hundred
hurricanes;[134]

day after day
I burn in the fires
of my own well-earned karmas:[135]

Let me sink
into the flood
of honey gushing from your cool
lotus feet.[136]

52

You shine, O Lord of Gods, on the banks
of the Garuḍa River,

the fruits of our desires
taken form.[137]

You are like a tusker in rut,
dripping fragrant ichor from its temples;[138]

with your two she elephants,
Lakṣmī, the Lotus Lady, and Medinī,
goddess Earth,
you crush the heaps of sins
of those who bow down before you
as if they were marshy beds
of lotus flowers.

Victory to you!
May you live long![139]

53

You possess infinite virtues, eternally free of faults;
supreme,[140] you are the clever destroyer of hells,[141]
the one and only Lord
of celestials;

the body of truth to those
who fall at your feet:[142]

And Veṅkaṭeśa, the poet, composing these verses
of praise[143] for You shines,
a singer of Truth![144]

Afterword

The *Devanāyakapañcāśat*, Veṅkaṭeśa's "Fifty(-Three) Verses for the Lord of Gods," begins with the traditional *maṅgalaśloka*, a verse in *mālinī* meter evoking the protection and grace of the god. Such *maṅgalaślokas* are thought to evoke, in almost material way—through the physicality of recitation, prosperity, happiness, and auspiciousness (*kuśalam*)—decidedly "this-worldly" religious virtues. Such prayers for worldly happiness, well-being, even longevity and prosperity, are common in the earliest strata of *stotra* literature, as Jan Gonda has observed.[145] In some cases whole *stotras* were composed as talismans or charms for good luck, wealth, or religious power. The Śrīvaiṣṇava *stotra* often expresses such a talismanic dimension in its initial first verse—normally a prayer in the benedictive (*āśir liṅ*) or precative form—and in the final *phalaśrutis,* concluding verses that describe the manifold benefits (fruits, *phalāḥ*) of reading, reciting, or studying the poem. In its collapse of all temporal reality—the past exploits of the god, present accessibility in the temple, and expectation of future unions—into what might be termed a "tempiternal moment," the space of the poem, chanted, read, or remembered, embodies sacred time, a literary repository of auspiciousness.[146]

Veṅkaṭeśa's poem in the "old tongue" contains many of themes we have already explored in the Tamil *prabandhams.*[147] Like the Tamil poems, Veṅkaṭeśa's Sanskrit *stotra,* while emphasizing divine impassiveness and transcendence, also places emphasis on this particular Vishnu's relative accessibility, in spite of the obvious dependence and unworthiness of the saint-poet lover. Here again we find asymmetry and intimacy in a delicate balance. Devanāyaka is certainly an awesome presence—the first verse paints a vivid picture of this "Lord of Gods" being worshiped by monarchs among the gods who drench his feet with nectar from the garlands on their crowns as they prostrate before him—though the poem also mirrors in greatest measure, in the form of the Sanskrit *stotra,* the *akam* world of intimacy and intimate address we saw in the Tamil *prabandhams.* Devanāyaka is a gracious, approachable king; we feel he is capable of responding to the lyric intensity of these verses. He is the one, as verse 8 describes, and the narrative of Tiruvahīndrapuram confirms, who drew the poet back to himself, "like a bird on a string," when he was leaving town, heading back to Kāñcī, camped one night near the river Peṇṇai. The energy of praises—for the gurus, the saint-poets, for Devanāyaka's wife, Hemabjavaḷḷī, the goddess Śrī of Tiruvahīndrapuram—focuses on a god who not only listens to the poet, a god the poet sees from a distance, but a god who can, ultimately, most intimately, become the praise itself, the very poetry of the poet, and, in a possession image, become the poet himself:

be *fit for,* be *fond of,* praise;

be the praise
and the praiser himself!

Familiar themes build slowly: passionate devotion to a god in whom the mind bathes, as in a "cool, sweet and brimming pool of deep water," in an allusion to sexual intercourse; a god who moves through time and space, "Primal Lord," knower of "origins and ends," who is present in the "very center of the Sun's circle," within the hearts of good people, and who dwells in this earthly shrine and the holy Medicine Hill, "girt by shrines," the serpent well and the river, and most concretely and beautifully, in the temple icon, whose jewels and weapons are material forms of fundamental cosmic and spiritual truths. With verse 14, after a litany of prayers for poetic power, for "mind" and the "goddess of speech," we enter into the long poem's center of gravity: a steady, stepwise, head-to-toe "delectation" or "relish" (*anubhava*) of the "lovely body" of god.

Seeing your lovely body whose splendor is made even more perfect
by each perfect
  limb,

enjoyed by your beloved wives with unblinking, astonished
  eyes, and sought out
by the jewels and weapons that adorn it
  to increase their own radiance,

my sight, O Lord of Gods,
is not sated with
  seeing!

Veṅkaṭeśa uses in this introductory verse to the *anubhava* an image that goes back both to the Vālmīki Sanskrit and Kampaṉ Tamil *Rāmāyaṇas,* and one that serves as the core image of this book: the beauty of Sītā's body that outstrips her jewels, a beauty that is sought by the jewels, and not the other way around.[148] Jewels merely hide the beauty of the body. He also introduces here a motif that will go through dozens of variations in the course of the description of the Lord's body, and that the very energy and sensual detail of the description will serve to compound almost to obsession: the unsated and insatiable thirst of eyes.[149] The very method of the *anubhava* "gives body," as it were, to the claim in this verse that the Lord's body gains in splendor with the new splendor of each and every limb, and that the object of our love is infinite, our desire endless. Such *anubhavas* form the very heart of Veṅkaṭeśa's religio-aesthetic vision.

Anubhava: *Enjoying the Body of Vishnu*

From the eighth to fourteenth centuries in south India, the trope of exaggerated sequential description is used in distinctive ways first by Tamil saint-poets (Āḻvārs), and later by Śrīvaiṣṇava Ācāryas composing in Sanskrit and Tamil, to describe the male bodies of temple images (*vigraha, mūrti, mēṉi*): the various standing, seated, and reclining images of the god Vishnu in a growing network of shrines that dot the landscape of Tamil Nadu. I have already noted that Śrīvaiṣṇava commentators call such foot-to-head or head-to-foot descriptions *anubhavas:* "experiences" or "enjoyments" of the body of the god. Sanskrit and Tamil *anubhavas* in Śrīvaiṣṇava literature are visionary pictures of the deity meant not only as a tool for systematic tantric-style visualizations (*dhyānāni*) but also, as devotional visions, they are meant also to inspire emotion (*bhāva; anubhava*), an atmosphere of "divine passion," a direct experience of amorous feeling through a refined erotic language inherited from Sanskrit *kāvya.*

Like the *waṣfs* of the Hebrew *Shir ha-shirim* (The Song of Songs), the Śrīvaiṣṇava *anubhava* is a language of overflowing joy, and one of the most potent vehicles of love-language in the literature.[150] In the rush of images, the concrete, particular object of contemplation, the temple icon, expands before one's eyes. The poets' similes, metaphors, and double entendres serve at times to dissemble the original object of gazing—a jeweled belt, a toe, a thigh, earrings, crown or navel—this, along with mythic and cultic associations from Purāṇic or Pāñcarātra liturgical texts, creates a complex composite image of a vigorously protean god, a god whose full revelation could almost be said to be "not yet" attained by the devotee-beholder.

Yet in spite of their lyrical energies and dissembling metaphors, such descriptive texts are decidedly rooted in an individual experience of a particular beloved form of Vishnu, a "cultic" context where one is honoring the temple body of a deity. The saint-poet's experience is shaped by the sanctum icons, by their individual liturgical service and ritual honor (*pūjā*).[151] Even when Vishnu is seen to change form, to move about like a living being, or to be played with like a doll (as in the charming narrative of the Muslim princess who fell in love with the plundered temple image of Raṅganātha), the poets often simply oscillate in imaginative vision between the immoble standing or reclining stone *mulabera* and the bronze festival images (*utsava mūrtis*) that stand before them in the "literal" space of the temple sanctum or as booty in the palace storerooms of a Delhi Sultan.[152] Vishnu in this southern Tamil and Sanskrit poetry is the god who stood/dwelt and is "standing/dwelling" (the verb *nil* is most commonly used in the Tamil verses)—he "dwelt/stood" (*niṉṟa*, past participle) and continues "dwelling/abiding/standing" (*niṉṟi*, forms of *nil* in the gerundive) in the temple and its environs, but most vividly "stands/abides" there right in front of the adoring poet, as the physical temple icon, even while he has, simultaneously, *become all things*. To the late poet and scholar A. K. Ramanujan, the paradigmatic verse that describes this telescoping experience, drawing together in dynamic tension the universal and particular object of desire, appears in the work of Nammāḻvār, one of the earliest and most treasured of Tamil saint-poets. Nammāḻvār's stanza reads almost like a grammatical paradigm, as Ramanujan notes, "a breathless recital of Tamil pronouns." In his concise translation:

We here and that man, this man,
  and that other in-between,
and that woman, this woman
  and that other, whoever,

Those people, and these,
  and these others in-between,
this thing, that thing,
  and this other in-between, whichever,

All things dying, these things,
  those things, those others in-between,
good things, bad things,
  things that were, that will be,

being all of them,
he stands there.[153]

Veṅkaṭeśa's *anubhavas* take this Tamil paradigm and play with it, play endlessly with images of Vishnu's terrific forms, telescoping all times, past, present, and future, myth and narrative history, universal and minute particular, dissembling and the singular focus, in one complex and extravagant act of beholding. That god who performed so many exploits in so many remote ages, who took on so many different forms, who *is*, simultaneously, so many very different things, he is also, perhaps above all, *here*, in the shrine, before the loving gaze of the saint-poet.

From verses 14 to 45, almost the entire length of the praise-poem, we enjoy the body of Devanāyaka from crown to eyes—their reddened corners—lips, ears, neck, chest shining with warrior's scars of bowstrings, belly, navel, thighs, knees, calves, and the quicksilver light of the toenails, source of the torrential Gaṅgā River.

The remaining verses (46–53) are an extended coda to the central movement of the *stotra* that "embodies the body" of god: the emphasis here is on unworthiness before such a vision, the inevitable asymmetry of the fragile and fallible human lover and the impassible and perfect beloved. Here we have the theme of the divided heart, and the belief in the talismanic force of rhetorical complaint and also praise that seeks, through its very excesses, to heal that divide. This is the meaning of the elaborate ritual surrender (*prapatti*) to Devanāyaka that ends this poem, along with others in this volume. Thief of his own body, a stolen anklet of a king, "emperor of worthless fools," the saint-poet here moves from a mood of abject surrender to final praises and a cosmic confidence that such skillfully composed verses and such elaborate self-effacement will make this singer "shine," a "singer of Truth" (*satyavādī*).

5

One Hundred Verses for the Invincible Lord of Medicine Hill: The *Acyutaśatakam*

1

Bow down before Acyuta,[1]
the Lord of Gods,
Lord of Truth to his servants,
inextinguishable radiance,
dark cool *tamāla* tree
on the banks of the Garuḍa River:

a king of elephants
who wanders the slopes of Medicine Hill
in the town
of the Serpent King.[2]

2

O Lord true to your servants
may this praise that I
a mere boy
composed
in the sweet lisping tongue
of Brahmā's
young wife

please you
like the prattling
of a caged parrot.[3]

3

Though my words are dirty,
O Lord true to your servants,
let them be clean,
touched by the streaming moonlight of your fame,

like ditchwater
draining
into the three-streamed
holy Gaṅgā.[4]

4

O Lord of Gods, let my poor song shine,
standing like a king's buffoon
in the midst of the Vedas:

those honored bards
in your assembly.

5

O Acyuta, sitting firm on the lion seat
of our teachers' tongues,
you expound the highest truth:

remove our ignorance.[5]

6

Like the full moon in the waves of Jāhnu's daughter
you shine
in the hearts of the teachers:

O Acyuta

like the goose that shuns turbid water
you do not enter
even for an instant
murky hearts.[6]

7

Your only authority is the Veda
yet your full glories
shine
in simple cowherd girls:

easy of access to those with faithful
hearts
O Lord who is truth to those who bow down
before you
you leave those who waver
uncertain
far behind in the dust.

8

O Lord true to those who surrender
hundreds of Upaniṣads
sing of you
as one who always shuns what needs shunning,
who is truth, knowledge
and joy
and who leaps beyond
the threefold ends
of time, space,
words, and things.[7]

9

Uncreated,
you create all things;
you sustain them,
unsustained by anything
other than yourself;
indestructible,
you destroy everything
leaving no trace behind:

You shine,
a seamless radiance
O Lord of Ahīndrapuram,
Town of the Serpent King.

10

Though you are the measure of an atom,
O Acyuta,
your power to support all things
is awesome.

This the Veda says:
you spread yourself everywhere,
filling every pore of existence
standing
fully present
in every thing.[8]

11

O Acyuta
everything that is
is your body;
you stand
as overlord
controller and support
of all things:

you yourself have shown
how you are both cause and effect
bound together
like two colors
woven into one garment.

This is why the Vedas call you
The All.

12

Having matter and souls as your body
O Acyuta,
you become the material cause
of worlds;
joined to your creative will
you also are
the efficient cause,
such is your inscrutable
power.[9]

13

Your play is the common cause of things
the same water
for a myriad of seeds:

distinctions
from Brahmā to a grass-blade
arise from the powers of
each thing's
karma.

14

Men are your manifest power,
O Acyuta;
those known as women
are Lakṣmī.
Except for you and her,
nothing else exists,
and even she is nothing but your radiance:
What else is there
to say?[10]

15

Nothing O Lord
either equals or exceeds you,
you are the sole refuge for all worlds:
to know this
O Lord of Gods,
is the essence of knowledge,
the end of all study.

16

The rich and abundant fruits
of your command,
O Lord of the Town
of the Serpent King,
are in plain sight for those who
follow it:

even Brahmā, Śiva,
and the others
can't overmaster
its power.[11]

17

Each ritual action
set down in the Vedic injunctions
points to you alone,
O Lord who is Truth to your slaves:
gods eat your leftovers
like holy brahmans, consecrated by mantras,
who play ancestors
at the death rituals.[12]

18

If you were not always present,
O Acyuta,
when the gods evoked in sacrifices
perish
at the end of each world-age,
who would bestow
the fruits of actions
in ages to come?

19

Like the wish-granting tree of Indra's Paradise
entwined with its golden
creeper,
the goddess Śrī,

O Lord true to those who bow to you,

you bestow all desired fruits:
your cool shade breaks
the relentless heat
of the three worlds.

20

You stand established as the end
of all the Vedas;
indwelling soul even of gods,
nourishing mother-spirit
of the fruits of all actions,
O Lord true to those who bow down to you,

showing no favor,
   are you not the same to all beings?[13]

21

But if you are so impartial to all,
   rooted in truth
      a fullness brimming over,
O Lord true to your slaves,

why then did you take sides with the Pāṇḍavas
   and their kind,
suffering even the role
   of a servant?[14]

22

For all those, O Lord
   their senses blasted, sickened,
who stumble, lost
   on the broken savage road
   of their karma,
there is no one but you,
   O Lord true to those who surrender,
to give them
a hand.

23

What is outside the scope of your knowing,
   O Acyuta,
beyond the reach of your mercy,
   what burden too heavy
for your strength?

Are you not then
the most perfect means
   to our most perfect end,
both the way and the goal?[15]

24

Are you not,
   O Lord true to your servants
a sturdy raft for souls

to cross
  the deep ocean of existence,
your will the ferryman,
your mercy,
  wind in the sail?

25

The other gods
who fancy themselves great lords of creation
  can't give us
release:
a thousand paintings of the suṅ
  do not
make night
  into day.

26

O Lord of Ahīndrapuram,
  ocean of holy nectar's sweetest essence,
the jewels of your auspicious qualities
  precious, pure
inaccessible to others,
  can't be counted.[16]

27

O Lord of the Town
  of the Serpent King
auspicious red streak in the hair-part
  of the Veda,
extreme limit of all good qualities,
destroyer of delusion
  stain, desire

you shine:

  a flame of dark sapphire
in the hearts of sages.[17]

28

You shine,
  your chest adorned with the mole,
its lovely curl of white hair,
and with Śrī,
  beyond parting,
even for an instant;

always hungry for war-cries,
  your glad sport,
you are an elephant in the forests
  near the banks
of the fertile Garuḍa River.

29

The Veda praises your body,
  O Lord of Ahīndrapuram,
  its ageless youth,
never having passed even into young
  manhood; a thing of beauty
and desire, eternal,
  befitting your Lordship,
self-manifest,
  your sweet happy body
honored by angels.[18]

30

The three strands of nature
  luminous, passionate, and dark
and their transformations;
  the cosmic man,
the totality of all things enumerated
  in the sacred texts:

are not all these the weapons and ornaments
  on your ethereal body?[19]

31

From you come
  the divine descents

heroes with powers to crush their cruel enemies,
reestablishing highest order:
the fruit of their actions
  is the protection
of good people.

32

A luster deepening its green the color of dark emerald,
  spreading along the borders of the town
of the Serpent King,

you are a monsoon cloud
  raining in season
  for your servants
mercy's
  sweet essence.[20]

33

You seem like the king of the elephants who guard
the compass-points. A delight to the eye
I see you

with your two she-elephants
  Lakṣmī and Bhū
in the forest marshes near the Garuḍa River,

tearing trees to their roots
  those demon chieftains
showering from your temples
  a heady ichor.[21]

34

The mass of dark hair between the sun of your crown
  and the moon
of your face,
  O Lord true to your servants,

fully reveals your power to make the incoherent
  cohere.[22]

35

Your face,
O Lord true to your servants
whose wide-open eyes
are like a pair of full-blown lotuses
shames the full moon:

merely to remember it is to destroy
even sins
knowingly done.

36

Your chest, O Acyuta,
lovely with its mole Śrīvatsa
and Lady Lakṣmī,

inseparable from its long chaplet of flowers,
made most auspicious
by Kaustubhā precious gem
of the Milk Ocean

and by sprays of cool holy basil,
praises your glory.

37

O Lord of Gods,
troupes of celestials fleeing the heat
with Brahmā at their head

enjoy the cool dense shade of the wish-granting tree
of your four
long arms.

38

How is your waist
still so thin,
when you hold in your stomach
the eggs
of worlds

like big bubbles on the ocean of primal matter
stirred to its depths
  by the moon
of your will?[23]

39

The lovely lotus sprung from your navel
with a black bee Brahmā
in its center,
O Lord of Serpent King town,

shines like the footstool of Lakṣmī
who sits on your chest.

40

Your yellow waist-cloth is streaked red with the blood
of Madhu and Kaitabha,
demons you crushed without mercy:

its girdle
whose bells are tinkling
  shines like golden fetters
for the lord of elephants,
  the mad God of Love.[24]

41

Your thighs,
  a bed for the Dānava chieftains'
long sleep of death seem,

O Lord true to your servants,

like twin high pillars supporting the three worlds
  that you hold
  in your belly.

42

A lover's beauty,
deepened by the emerald ladles of your shins
and the twin jeweled mirrors
of your knees,

O Acyuta,

never leaves your feet
  that bear the marks of the lotus
like Lakṣmī.[25]

43

Your lotus foot,
  blossoming at the summit of the Veda,
a refuge for all creatures,
  shines,
O Lord true to those who surrender:

from it streamed the heavenly Gaṅgā
  born the moment you measured
the worlds,
  extinguishing the sins
  of the three-
fold universe.

44

Thus those without fault taste your sweetness
  taste you
who are divine nectar's very essence,[26]
root of all three worlds:

You appeared on the slopes of Medicine Hill like an herb
  that heals the wounds
of your servants.

45

Those who paint their eyes with your dark body
as with a mystical eye-black conjured by *siddhas,*[27]

O Acyuta,

see you
  as they would a treasure:
the ever-secret hiding-place of Lakṣmī.

46

You are the one sun of all three worlds,
  Lord of Planets

whose bright light cuts through
deepest darkness:

for those who see you there can be no night
of delusion.[28]

47

Your pure devotees O Acyuta
who have lost their taste
for the pleasures
of the senses,

indifferent to all
that
being born
passes away:

they live in their bodies as if already free
of this world.[29]

48

The soul,
that elephant always crazy with rut,
caught by you,

O Lord True to those who surrender

forgets its muddy forest streams,
forgets wealth
like a dream,
forgets cities drawn by clouds
on the air.

49

Those who know think little of the starry realms of Brahmā
and the others,

those places like the bubbles and spume of waves or clouds,
the soft stems of plantain

or the frail roots of white-flowering *kandalī*

thick in fields
after rain.[30]

50

Those noble men
   who can see into their own essential nature
as well as that of others,
         with compassion,

O Lord, Truth to those who submit,

   wearing your virtues,
could they ever let go of their lovingkindness
   for all beings?

51

O Lord true to your servants,
   self-conceit, lust, greed, deceit, envy,
   fear, anger,
   the jealous,
children of infatuation,
   stains born of delusion:
these are not seen
   in your devotees.[31]

52

Those who turn their hearts to other gods
spend all their time
in this black Kali age,

but to those,
   O Lord of Serpent King town
who hold to your feet

where did this dark age go?[32]

53

Those fools whose destruction
   is close as breath,
O Acyuta,
   see only faults in your men
who walk the good road
   of those who long for liberation

like the dying see holes in the circle
   of the sun.[33]

54

Like the sky free of dark clouds of ego,
  luminous with a mass of stars,
your spotless virtues,
  or flooded in the moonlight
of your tender loving,
  your devotees
  shine.

55

They surrender at your lotus foot,
  O Lord of Truth,
they'll never go to Yama's hell:

even if they stumble and fall they'll get off light,
a punishment suited to their high place

like servants in the king's
inner rooms.

56

They tremble with fear
O Acyuta,
  those who see the terrible knitted
brows
of the Lord of Ends quivering
  like a she-serpent;

filled with sorrow over sins caused by their own bad karma,

letting the sweet taste of sense pleasures
  slip away,
they worship
  your feet.

57

Even worship offered by Brahmā himself,
  Lord of all Creatures,
  clings to your feet
  alone:

you place on your own head like a holy
  ritual cloth

the offerings of those who love you
with one-pointed
love.

58

You never turn from those devotees
O Acyuta,
whose minds like moonstone that sweats
under shining
moonlight,

melt into a flood of tears at the sight
of your face,

whose bodies bristle their hairs standing on end like *kadamba* trees
bristle with buds
after a storm.[34]

59

Your devotees,
holding no hatred for anyone,
O Lord of those who seek refuge,
cleaving fast to your eternal law,
giving up all clinging,
they alone
reach you,
so difficult
to reach by
everybody else.

60

O Lord of the Town of the Serpent King,
those whose minds and hearts
wander, clinging
to things of this world,
even though they desire you,
can't obtain
you:
though you are near, always
you are hard
to grasp

like the air
we breathe.

61

Your devotees,
who have for so long thirsted for release,
yet filled with the taste
for your service,
O Acyuta,
hold fast to their bodies
held in thrall here
by you
who relish
the desire to protect the whole
world.[35]

62

We see them like walking dams made of mountains,
congealed forms
of your changeless virtues,
bridges for all things
moving and unmoving:

O Lord of those who submit,
by them all people can cross
the waters
of endless births.

63

Your devotees
have quelled their fears of another birth,
seeing each thing that
happens to them as good,
O Lord true to those who surrender:

they honor their last days
like a welcome guest.

64

In this world of growing gloom,
those who have made their mark,

are lamps
of perfect knowledge,
  trimmed and lit
by masters:

          and they are lead by you
always
  to your very own place
self-luminous,
  lit by no lamp.

65

They gaze at you with eyes
  of pure fixed
devotion:

in intimate union with you,
  O Lord of the Town of the Serpent King,

they fill the rows of heaven
  marked for the Serpent Lord himself
and the others
  who serve you.

66

Even kings like Mucukunda and Kṣetrabandu,
  sick of delays,
interminable stages on the ladder
  of contemplative
union, took refuge
  in you,
  so easy of access,
and were free.[36]

67

This creature thought by the gods
  to be merely the equal of a sacrificial animal,
O Lord of Gods,
  when he reaches your place
he is forever
  given ritual tribute
by all those,

divine or human,
who drown in the seas of births
and deaths.[37]

68

Your divine glance
O Acyuta,
sets fire to the great night of Māyā
flooded by dark seas of black delusion;
sets us firm
on our first course
in the long journey
to liberation.

69

To chant your name is to taste sweet nectar,
O Lord true to your servants:

it's the root of the tree of freedom's bliss,
best of the great elixirs
to cure the aging of delusion,

the one fertile soil
of auspiciousness.[38]

70

Worship of you,
even though cut short
left undone,
is never in vain
it will not lead to sin;

even the smallest act
done for you,
O Acyuta,
protects
from the greatest of fears.[39]

71

The other gods,
graceless

without your grace;
  in your grace alone are they gracious:[40]

what's the use of these gods we must worship
whose powers rest
  on your favor?

72

O Lord true to your servants,
what good will they do for me,
  these other gods
so pleased with my offerings:

a hundred clouds of mist
  can't quench

the great thirst
  of the *cātaka* bird.[41]

73

O Acyuta,
my thirst,
  an animal hungry for mirages of pleasure,
is quenched by the flood
  from your streams
      of grace

drenching with its torrents
those who seek
  your shelter.

74

Holding high
  my proud banner of duties,
mind-numbing ancillary rites
  hardest to perfect,
but badly done
  or botched,

I am really the man who stumbles lost,
  paralyzed by fear
  on backroads of desert
  wastes.

75

Though I cover my body in the armor of strictest law
I lead the army of outlaws:

My repentance is a joke.

No wonder you laugh at me when you are alone
with Lakṣmī.[42]

76

All time is not enough
to wipe away sins done in this body
even in one day:
O Acyuta,
I'm the perfect vessel
for your mercy.

77

O Acyuta,
your virtues and my faults
are equally immeasurable,

yet your virtues win:

is it their secrecy their stealth
that accounts
for their great
weakness?

78

My span of life is like a stand of trees
being cut
into
small pieces
day and
night:

even seeing this
my mind
is arrogant.

Hold gently O Acyuta
this simple
child.

79

Though the body,
the length of its breath a mystery,
its senses faltering
growing old
is like a rain-drop on the eaves of a house,

O Lord of those who surrender:

you know how I thirst
for long youth.

80

I'm ashamed, O Lord true to your slaves
I don't know what
to do;

and even if I should come to know what to do
quite by accident
I'll do the opposite:[43]

Is it right to abandon
me?

81

Who am I? What should I do?
What should I not
do? Only you have the power
to answer me,
you know it all:

Do right by me O Lord of gods
keep me
in your heart.

82

This body has been and will always be
like a wooden puppet
moved by threads

at the mercy
of somebody else:

be of good will to this body of mine tugged this way and that

by action speech
and mind,

O Lord of gods.[44]

83

Cutting the twin fetters of my karmas,
giving the good to my friends
and the bad
to those who hate me,

when O Acyuta

will you free me from this hole
of a prison-house
my cruel
body?[45]

84

When, O Acyuta, will you see me as your beloved child,
letting me rest in you
who dwell in my heart
before I catch on to the sun's rays
and climb up
the narrow artery
of Brahmā
to heaven?[46]

85

O Acyuta,
when will your men,
fleet guides along our journey
with Agni ahead and Amānava,
Lord of Lightning,
behind,
lead me across the wilderness waste
of threefold nature
clotted with darkness?[47]

86

When,
O Lord of those who surrender,

will you give me,
your servant,
my eternal lovely body
of light?[48]

When will I put on the ornaments of highest deity
and cross
the Viraja River?[49]

87

When O Lord of Gods will you pull me out of the sea
of birth and death,
cleansing my vision,
making a place for me over your heart

like the jewel Kaustubhā who sits on your chest
a hand-mirror
for Lakṣmī?

88

When will I be at your lotus foot,
O Lord true to your servants,
that spanned
in play
the three worlds:

exuding the torrential honey of the heavenly Gaṅgā,

that adorned the matted hair
of Śiva
killer of the love god?[50]

89

When will I become,
O Lord true to your slaves,
like one of your angelic icons,[51]
your beloved slave,

claiming as a crown for my head your two lotus feet,
blossoms that crown
the head of the Upaniṣads?

90

When, O Lord of gods,
   though I am fit never to return
to this world
   will you enjoy me
as one of your blessed friends on this earth
in the divine play
   of your incarnations,

equal to you if only in
   pleasure?[52]

91

There,
I've let my desire be known.

Utterly dependant upon you
   with these words
my essence:

Make them true,
   O Lord true to your slaves,
by your mass of auspicious
   powers:

you can do anything you want.

92

Like a baby monkey running in circles,
   eager to leap across the sea
because it was born
   of the race of Maruti,

I ask you:

O Acyuta whose lotus feet
all beings desire,
   indulge this,
   my monkey nature.

93

Overcome by sense objects
   I sink into the strong whirlpools
of the ocean of beings:

pull me out with your own hands
  O Acyuta,

nurse me back to health
  like a mother
  her sucking child.[53]

94

Scorched by the hot season of karmas,
none of my pleasures,
  those mere mirages,
gives as much as a drop
  of water:

Cool me O Acyuta with the winter hail
of your glances.

95

Freeing me from the blank stares of those who never think of you
  their eyes like poison,
  let fall on me,

O Acyuta,

the hard showers of your devotees' eyes
  the cool nectar
of their faces.

96

My heart wallows in gifts worthless as straw,
like honey mixed with poison:
stripped of I
    and mine,
fix this heart within you,
O Acyuta,
  treasure of nectar.

97

Put your two feet,
  O Lord true to those who surrender,

on the head of this eternal worthless fool,
 those feet
 precious as hidden
 treasure:

the fever of those who surrender is broken by cool rivers of light
 flowing
 from their toes!

98

If even after so many say I have surrendered to you,
you still don't protect me:

are your words not merely like the noise of waves
on the shore of the
sea?

99

O Lord, having no other refuge,
I've been entrusted to you
by gentle teachers
 full of mercy:

 seeing them,
 your dear ones,
O Lord true to those who surrender,

firmly bear the burden
 of my soul.[54]

100

O Lord true to those who surrender,
 take me back
 like the king
his young son,
 the prince who lived among crude hunters,
snatched back from the *caṇḍāla* village
on the advice of his ministers:

take me like the groom takes his young
bride-to-be.

101

May these hundred elegant stanzas for Lord Acyuta,
filled with all fine qualities,
composed by Veṅkaṭeśa
whom they call Vedāntācārya,
a lion among poets
and philosophers,
shine in the hearts
of the connoisseurs.[55]

Afterword

The *Acyutaśatakam* (One Hundred Verses for the Invincible Lord of Medicine Hill), Veṅkaṭeśa's long Māhārāṣṭrī Prākrit poem in *āryā* meter written for Devanāyaka at Tiruvahīndrapuram, expresses in striking ways all of the themes we have touched in upon in our discussion of the *Devanāyakapañcāśat* in Sanskrit, though in a simpler, less elaborate style suitable to the lyric registers of its language. The Prākrit poem, though it is a long and complex theological/philosophical summary, foregrounds intimate emotional and erotic motifs of lack and of striving, and embodies a certain elegance and simplicity native to this literary tongue. The use of a single meter—the hallowed *āryā* of the ancient Prākrit *gāthās*—that resists embedded phrases and extensive ornamentation (*alaṃkāra*) also works to hone down expression. As Martha Ann Selby has noted, the "structural brevity" of the *āryā* meter has led Prākrit poets "to explore avenues other than those found in more conventional 'representational' or 'mimetic' techniques for conveying meaning." The emphasis in the Prākrit verses is not on "surface tensions" or elaborate visible registers of mimetic meaning, but on what Selby calls a "poetics of anteriority," a "plurality of semiotic referents" that exist not in the text "on the page" but "somewhere outside of it," "anterior" to it.[56] Classical Māhārāṣṭrī Prākrit is often a miracle of conciseness and simplicity, evoking a world of emotions and abstract ideas in the most economical fashion, and Veṅkaṭeśa's Prākrit is no exception.

Māhārāṣṭrī is a southern literary Prākrit with obvious links to the Dravidian languages, particularly Tamil of the *caṅkam* period (ca. first to third centuries C.E.). As Selby has noted, according to Prākrit grammarians, Māhārāṣṭrī is "Prākrit *par excellence*," its most perfect and polished form.[57] In the hands of centuries of great poet-dramatists, Māhārāṣṭrī Prākrit was a prestigious tongue of refined emotions, and is a poetic language that plays a crucial role in the formulation of Indian aesthetic theories after the ninth-century Kashmiri poet and theorist Ānandavardhana.

Ultimately, it should come as no surprise by now that Veṅkaṭeśa, the consummate virtuoso artist in Sanskrit and Tamil, the "lion among poets and philosophers," would chose such a prestigious form of Prākrit to compose this hymn to Devānayaka. His hundred verses in "heart-captivating" Prākrit (*cintaikavar pirākiruta*), meant to "shine in the hearts of connoisseurs," only add to the already rich south Indian textures of his poetic work.

At the very end of the *Acyutaśatakam* (verse 101), Veṅkaṭeśa asks that

> ... these hundred elegant stanzas for Lord Acyuta
> filled with all fine qualities,
> composed by Veṅkaṭeśa
> whom they call Vedāntācārya,
> a lion among poets and philosophers,
> shine in the hearts
> of the connoisseurs.

It is thus that this Māhārāṣṭrī Prākrit—Saravatī's charming "mother-tongue," the language of Kālidāsa and Hāla before him—becomes, from now on, also the Prākrit of Veṅkaṭeśa's hymns to Vishnu at Tiruvahīndrapuram, touched by the manifold influences of this polyglot religious artist. It is up to those of "like heart" (the *sahṛdayāḥ*: connoisseurs) to make the connections.

Asymmetry and Intimacy: Veṅkaṭeśa's Dialectic of Love

The overall structural asymmetry noted in other praise-poems in this book holds true here as well, in even more compact, concrete, and vivid form. The poem, in simple and powerful verses, begins in humble supplication, evoking unworthiness, ignorance, and lack in the saint-poet, and the infinite superiority of the object of praise, the beloved god. Then, from the oppositions of the poet's "ditch-water" to the god's "three-streamed holy Gaṅgā," from the "buffoon" lover with his young girl-child's tongue to the beloved who shines, a "seamless radiance," the poem builds toward a powerful visionary joy-in-presence in the *anubhava*, of extravagant beholding and exuberant praise. The very force of the language seems to leap the gulf between lover and beloved. After the crescendo of the *anubhava*, holding together in tension divine particularity and ideality, concrete presence and transcendence, poem and saint-poet alike slowly deliquesce again into complaint and lament, presentational vision liquefies, and we have again the weepy, vulnerable, all-too-human lover, reaching—but now into silence—or mere chaos, "the noise of waves on the shore of the sea." But again, as in the *Devanāyakapañcāśat,* the power of the language itself is, at the end, a guarantee that, in spite of the weaknesses of its poet, the praise-poem is bound to hit its mark and become a "pretext" for the beloved's mercy. At least this will be obvious to the "connoisseurs."

Redescription and Surprise

Individual verse translations here differ formally in some places, though not in content or choice of words, from those selected in my larger study of Veṅkaṭeśa, *Singing the Body of God.*[58] As we noted in the Introduction, translation for many, like poetry itself, is an ongoing process: this collection, its style, logic, and voice, is a slice of intellectual time, a biographical moment in the translator's creative and scholarly life, a river flow caught in the image of another language, both refracting and reflecting, redescribing and reinscribing, the "original."

I hope that those readers who can go back to the original will go back with a new sense of the particular power of this lyric form, inspired by the peculiar surprises and also, to return to the vocabulary of J. Z. Smith, the incongruities of translation.[59] I hope that those who do not know how to read Prākrit are inspired to do so. For both, I would like these translations, and all translations in this volume, to serve as poems in their own right, extending the Veṅkaṭeśa tradition of devotion into American English.

6

At Play with Krishna in the Tamil Land: The *Gopālaviṃśati*

1

His shining body lights up the woods of Vṛndāvana;[1]
cherished lover of the simple cowherd girls,[2]
he was born on Jayantī
		when Rohiṇī touches,
	on the eighth day,
the waning moon in Āvaṇi:[3]
		this luminous power[4] that wears Vaijayantī
the long garland of victory,

I praise Him![5]

2

We see him as he fills with delight,
	on his very own lap,
Sarasvatī, goddess of Speech;[6] as he raises to his lotus lips
	the royal conch shell,
	Pāñcajanya.

			Seated firm in a lotus flower
set in the center
	of a shining yantra of many colors,[7]

	praise him,

great monarch of cowherds.[8]

3

His lower lip trembles
as he begins
to cry—
the air fills
with the fragrance
of Veda;

at one moment

he is all sweet smiles,

then
suddenly
his eyes
fill with tears:[9]

I know him,
the one who took on the tiny infant body of a cowherd[10]
who sucked the milk
and the very life-breath[11]
from the false mother Pūtanā:
I know this Gopāla,
the Cowherd King,
as Most High
Supreme Being![12]

4

May I see it with my own eyes:

first,
the threshing ring
of jeweled anklets—[13]

the raised leg,
bent,
one foot,

turning in the air!

—the other firm
on the floor—

then the throbbing
clipped
rhythms

to the thwacking ruckus
of churning
curds![14]

—this sweet butter dance of the Lord
in Nanda's
house.

5

Plunging his little hand deep into the big jar
he steals sweet
new butter
fresh from the churning:[15]

then, seeing his mother come running,
burning with anger,
a rope
in her hand,

he neither flees nor stands still,
but trembling,
just a little,[16]

and squinting,
quickly closes
his eyes:

Protector of the World,
clever false cowboy,[17]
may He protect us.

6

He is stung by sharp sidelong glances of the Vraj girls;
treasure of Mathurā, sweetest enjoyment
for those who love
no other.

I sing of that inconceivable supreme *Brahman*[18]

—who can know it?
we see it
suckling at the breasts of Vasudeva's wife,
playing in the lovely body
of this charming
young boy.

7

He twists his neck backward
out of fear,
then the bud
of his pouting lower lip
blooms
into a smile:

I recall in silence[19]
that young prince

who drags the big mortar
through the garden
and tearing the trees from their roots
frees
the two spirits.

8

I see him here always
before my eyes.[20]
This lovely boy
whom even the highest wisdom
of the Veda
seeks to have
by its side:

the two Arjuna trees
were witness
to his childish pranks
and the Yamunā
the long days
of his youth.[21]

9

You are the shortest path to liberation,
a dark monsoon cloud that hangs over the forest
raining
joy and wealth.[22]

A bamboo flute thrills at the touch
of your ruddy
lower lip:[23]
I love you and worship you,[24]
root cause of creation,
pure compassion
in the body
of a man.[25]

10

We must honor him with unblinking eyes:
eternally youthful,[26] his curly locks of black hair
vie in battle

with the black eyes
of peacock feathers:

may this luminous beauty whose intensity
maddens my senses[27]

be always
present
in my mind.

11

The sweet reed flute calls them,
sending every cowgirl
it touches
with its music
into ecstasies;[28]
the flood of his glancing
eyes

red lilies
in the river of his mercy

cooled by his flawless
  smile:[29]

may He protect me.

12

The lovely reed flute that presses against his lower lip;
the garland of peacock feathers
that adorn his crown;

  a darkness luminous
as shards of cool
  blue
    sapphire:[30]

may these glorious visions[31]
  appear
    before my eyes
at my journey's
  end.

13

Each and every hour—
    waking or sleeping—[32]
I gaze on the beauty of this young man
with Lady Lakṣmī on his chest

who is loved
    by the long-limbed girls of Vraj—
his beauty[33]
  far beyond the scope
of my singing.[34]

14

What artist has painted this young man in my heart[35]
who wears in his hair the lovely feathers

of a peacock

who is the sun
to the lotus faces of the cowgirls of Vraj
sick with love?[36]

15

With head bowed low
  hands pressed together
in prayer

I salute

  this luminous darkness
shining black as *kohl*
    under women's eyes:[37]

he plays a lovely flute
  that breathes
in tune
  with the lisping bangles[38]

of the cowherd girls
  crazy
in love.

16

The cowherd girls' hands
  clap the beats

      cooled by the touch of their slinking
            loose
bangles[39]

as they teach the flute
    the graceful *lalitā*
      dance.

Hail to that flute

    that shares sweet nectar
from the lips
    of Vishnu,
        red as coral,

      who took the form
of a cowherd boy
    to protect
        the whole world!

17

On his ears hang rings of *lāṅgalī* flowers;[40]
his dark hair shines
with feathers
of a peacock and thick red *bandhujīva*[41]
blossoms; on his chest,
the long necklace of yellow *guñjā*-beads:[42]

praise him, who is adorned in so many ways,
some strange kind of Trickster[43]
who steals

            the youth
of the cowherd
girls.

18

He holds the playful shepherd's crook in the tender sprout[44]
of his right hand; his other hand
   fondles the slender
shoulders
   of the lady
         who thrills at his touch,
                  the hairs on her body

      shining,

            stand erect.[45]

Lovely, dark as the monsoon cloud, his flute tucked into the folds
   of his yellow waist-cloth, and his hair shimmering
with garlands
   of *guñjā*-
beads,

      praise Him,
tender lover of the *gopīs*.[46]

19

He gazes at his lover,
   her eyes
            half-

closed
in ecstacy,

whom he embraced
from behind—

his hands tightly
circling
the curve of her waist—

as she struck a pose to shoot
the sweet water.[47]

In one hand
he grasps his own long syringe,[48]

and with the other
he cinches
tight
his dress

for water-sports:[49]

cherished lover of simple cowherd girls,[50]
good life-giving medicine
for the devotees,[51]

may he protect us.

20

After stealing the cowherd girls' dresses as they lay
strewn along the banks
of the Yamunā,
bright river daughter of the Sun,[52]

smiling playfully,[53]

he sat in the branches of a lovely Kunda tree.

And when, burning with shame,
they pleaded
for their clothes,

he commanded they come,
one by one,
out of the water,

their lotus hands raised high
over their
heads
in prayer:

Praise this fabulous lover,
this god
in love.[54]

21

Those who study with one-pointed mind this praise-poem
composed by Veṅkaṭeśa
will see before their very eyes
this inconceivable unknowable god[55]
who is so dear to young girls,
deft connoisseur
of the holy reed
flute![56]

Afterword

Standing on top of the hill overlooking the temple and the gentle curve of the blue Garuḍa River in the Tamil land, one must imagine, as the sacred biographies do, that the saint-poet can hear the happy noise of churning curds and the tinkling of anklets.[57] Through the air redolent with jasmine sound the long and lovely notes of a flute, the shrieking and laughter of girls in a village tank, and the sad painful howling of the demonness Pūtanā. Northern Mathurā and the dark mythical forests of Vṛndāvana are *here* in Veṅkaṭeśa's religious imagination, at this hallowed place in south India, Tiruvahīndrapuram, looped by areca and coconut groves and fields of paddy: Krishna the God-King looks out from the consecrated wide-open eyes of the standing image of Lord Vishnu Devanāyaka in his dim sanctum lit by ghee-lamps and heavy with the odors of camphor and champak and *kasturi*.

It is said that Veṅkaṭeśa spent long hours on this hill below the temple near the Hayagrīva shrine, meditating on Vishnu/Krishna, Māyōṉ, Trickster Lord of Jasmine, visualizing his mantras, mentally entering a yantra spread with red flowers: he had mentally constructed his images of the Lord with Sarasvatī on his lap, felt his poetic and spiritual powers wax and dazzle. But one night something else happened, something more than ritual graces, or the inevitable results of polished, disciplined meditation and practice of Pāñcarātra rites. Late one night, long after evening worship, while he stood before the Devanāyaka image in Tiruvahīndrapuram temple, he was beheld by the god, and so transported to another world, to the Krishna-world within that image of Vishnu. And held in thrall by that gaze, he saw with his "devotional eye," and he sang what he saw in verses of exquisite Sanskrit.

Though all forms of Lord Vishnu are here in this temple image, and unfold in serried theological array before his willing singers—the Boar and the Warrior Brahman, Tortoise, Man-Lion, and Dwarf, Buddha and Rāma—that evening the poet Veṅkaṭeśa was struck by the luminous beauty of the Lord's most sweet and accessible form as Krishna, the cowherd and king, handsome Kaṇṇaṉ, lover of *gopīs* and child-prince of thieves from the forests of Vṛndāvana.

It is said that then he composed this poem, the *Gopālaviṃśati*, at Tiruvahīndrapuram. After praising the manifold forms and powers and exploits of Vishnu as Devanāyaka in Sanskrit, Tamil, and Māhārāṣṭrī poems of great power and theological sophistication—poems we have had a chance to read in translation in this book—he also sang this praise of Vishnu as Krishna come down from the north. This is a Krishna, however, who had, from an early time, already entered Tamil consciousness as the god of the jasmine landscape.

Krishna in a World of Vishnu

In the Tamil religious literature of south India, Krishna rarely stands alone as an object of devotion. In the poetry of saint-poets, from the earliest Tamil Āḻvārs around the eighth to tenth centuries, to the Sanskrit *stotras* of Ācāryas from the twelfth to the fourteenth centuries, Krishna comes, as it were, layered with other forms (*avatāras* or "incarnations") of Vishnu. As Vidya Dehejia has noted, even in the *tirumoḻis* of the female Āḻvār Āṇṭāḷ, one of the most passionate poets of Krishna the Cowherd Lover, Krishna and Vishnu are "not sharply differentiated."[58] Krishna in Āṇṭāḷ is a composite god who mirrors various forms of Vishnu, whether it be the cosmic form of Raṅganātha asleep on the Ocean of Milk between creations, Vāmana the Dwarf who spanned and measured the worlds, Narasiṃha the "Man-Lion," the Boar, or Rāma of the *Rāmāyaṇa*. There are also complex allusions to the ancient Tamil deity of the "jasmine landscape" (forest or pasture), the *pāvai* rites for rain and fertility performed by young women in the month of Mārkaḻi, and other references that place this "Krishna" squarely within a specifically Tamil literary and cultural landscape.[59] Vasudha Narayanan in *The Way and the Goal*, her study of devotion in early Śrīvaiṣṇava tradition, makes this argument also for Periyāḻvār, another well-known Tamil saint-poet of Krishna. She notes the oscillation between Rāma and Krishna in various verses of the *Periyāḻvār Tirumoḻi*, including a set of game songs wherein the poet volleys back and forth with praises of each form of Vishnu, ending with a signature verse wherein both forms, Rāma and Krishna, are praised in one breath equally: "Nanda's son and Kākutstha."[60] One of the most vivid and charming evocations of the child Krishna in Āḻvār Tamil literature and the later Sanskrit *stotras* of the Ācāryas is of the child-god tied (impossibly!) to a mortar by a "tight-knotted string" (*kaṇṇinuṇciṟuttāmpu*). An extended meditation on this image is in the *Atimānuṣa Stava* of Kūrattāḻvāṉ, where the butter-thief of Yaśodā's house, his hair smeared with the mud of grazing cows, is inseparable in the poet's vision from other *avatāras* of Vishnu, for they are all present before the poet's eyes in the temple image of Vishnu (the *arcāvatāram*), the supreme center of gravity of most Tamil and Sanskrit poems in early Vaiṣṇava literature.[61]

This kind of layering, where "Krishna" is but one form of Vishnu being praised, even in verses dominated by images of the Cowherd Boy or the Mountain Lifter, is also common in the Sanskrit *stotras* and Tamil *prabandhams* of Veṅkaṭeśa. Verse 9 from his Tamil *Meyviratamāṉmiyam* (to Varadarāja Perumāḷ at Kāñcī) is characteristic of this multiple layering: first we have Rāma, then the child-god Krishna, then, in a funneling motion, an evocation of place and specific temple *arcāvatāram* (here Varadarāja Perumāḷ at Kāñcī):

The hero
  who felled in one cluster
the ten heads
  of the well-armed demon
with an arrow
  let loose
from the lovely graceful bow
  fitted
for the exalted field
  of battle;

      our great father
who ate the sweet butter spread
on the surface

of brimming jars fit
for churning:

he is here,
on Elephant Hill,
that cuts to the root
more cleanly
than his Discus—
that mere ornament—
the sins
of the devotees![62]

In the Sanskrit *stotra* to Devanāyaka Swāmi at Tiruvahīndrapuram, amid verses filled with allusions to every *avatāra*, there comes this verse that could have almost come out of Āṇṭāḷ:

O Lord of immortals, mad with love,
my mind kisses your lower lip red as *bimbā* fruit,
as the tender young shoots
from the coral tree
of paradise:

your lips enjoyed by young cowherd girls,
by your flute

and by the prince
of conch shells.[63]

This being said, Veṅkaṭeśa also wrote in Sanskrit some distinguished poetry focused on Krishna and *Kṛṣṇalīlā* alone. First, there is his long *mahākāvya* on the "life" of Krishna, the *Yadavābhyudayam* or "Glory of the Yadavas," and second, the *stotra* translated here, the *Gopālaviṃśati*, a cycle of twenty verses (plus a *phalaśruti* or concluding signature verse) for Gopāla, the Cowherd God.

A Praise-Poem for Krishna as "Lord of Gods"

The *Gopālaviṃśati* is a praise-poem (*stotra*), and not a *kāvya*. It has a rich liturgical history at Devanāyaka Swāmi Temple, which includes its use as a marriage hymn and as a blessing over food offered to the temple image (the *tadīyārādhanam*). On Krishna Jayantī, the image (*mūrti*; *arcā*) of Devanāyaka is taken in procession to the chanting of this hymn. As we have already seen,

Veṅkaṭeśa composed for Devanāyaka another very important Sanskrit *stotra*, two Tamil *prabandhams*, and one long Māhārāṣṭrī Prākrit *stotra*.[64] They are distinctive in their passionate devotion to this particular form of Vishnu, for their use of the first person and various erotic motifs from Sanskrit literature and *akam* conventions of classical love poetry in ancient Tamil. It thus comes as no surprise that Veṅkaṭeśa identified this particularly beloved form of Vishnu as Gopāla, the sensuously evocative and emotionally accessible cowherd youth and god of the Vṛndāvana pastorale.

This comparatively short *stotra* gives the reader a vivid sense of Krishna in the Tamil land. It includes set descriptions and "enjoyments" of the body of Krishna that are meant to inspire devotional feeling (*bhāva*) in the hearer, and to downplay love's drama of asymmetry and intimacy. The poem is like an extended ecstatic *anubhava*, a presentational vision that averts its gaze from the many tensions between lover and beloved that we see in the other *stotras* and *prabandhams* in this volume. Here Veṅkaṭeśa places emphasis on the ecstatic poesis of wondrous beholding, muting the asymmetries of love, human and divine. The divine "person" of Krishna seems to soften, by his overwhelmingly gentle presence, the borders of saint-poet beholder and divine object of his love.

We move in Veṅkaṭeśa's Krishna poem from the cosmological, in the evocation of the birth date, to ritual forms of meditation, the shining yantra of many colors; soon we are at the heart of the emotional *imaginaire* of Vṛndāvana pastorale, where the transcendent *Brahman*, inconceivable, unknowable, formless Being has become a tiny cranky baby, a toddler butter thief and trickster, a dancer in the courtyard, a flute-playing cowherd, a merciless killer of demons, a handsome lover who plays at concealing and revealing his divine power.

Like so many poets in south Indian bhakti tradition from the earliest period, Veṅkaṭeśa delights in juxtaposing the Lord's awesome extremes: the Big and the Little, Child and Primal Being, Unknown God and intimate Friend and Lover, extremes that meet in this God of Love, and *in* love (*kāmī*).

7

Praises of Devanāyaka by Tirumaṅkaiyā̲lvār: From the *Periyatirumo̲li*

Devanāyaka is not generally singled out by the Ā̲lvārs as a particular object of intense love, nor is the "Town of the Serpent King"—unlike Veṅkaṭam, Kāñcī, or Śrīraṅgam—singled out as a particularly important site in the development of the Ā̲lvār cultus. Veṅkaṭeśa has gone his own way with this form of Vishnu, which makes these poems seem more personal than others in his oeuvre.

Of all the Ā̲lvārs, only Parakāla, the Ā̲lvār from Tirumaṅkai (ninth century, also known as Kalikan̲r̲i, Kalivairī, Kaliyan̲, Nīla, and Tirumaṅkaiyā̲lvār) has written of this shrine and its icon, but in a style quite different from Veṅkaṭeśa's.[1] Parakāla's praise of Tiruvahīndrapuram is written in the genre of Tamil strophic songs called *tirumo̲li*. The *tirumo̲li* is very different in feel and conventional expression from later *prabandhams* like the *Mummaṇikkōvai*; it has less metrical and motivic variety, and is more formulaic and repetitive, with song-like refrains praising the town and the riches of the landscape. The main body of the *tirumo̲li* consists of nine songs and a *śrutiphala*, the end-verse that promises merit and even the destruction of sins both for the singer and for the reader/listener. And like Veṅkaṭeśa's *Gopālaviṃśati*, its mode is pure praise.

Parakāla's poem is scintillating in its word-pictures: the flora and fauna of the sacred hill, the river Garuḍa, the fertile plains and fields of ripe paddy. His Tamil is less overtly theological than Veṅkaṭeśa's, more vividly in touch with minute particulars; as a poet the Ā̲lvār is more in touch with the lyric riches of Tamil, particularly in his use, in other poetry cycles, of folk genres and game songs. His surfaces dazzle in ways never matched by Veṅkaṭeśa's *prabandhams*. Parakāla links the place and its landscape to the four classical *tiṇai* of the *caṅkam* corpus in ways never matched in Veṅkaṭeśa's later work. When we hear of the *mātavi*—a type of jasmine blossom—we can be confident that the poet wants us to think of the *mullai tiṇai*, or "jasmine landscape," whose corresponding emotional state is "patient waiting"; when we hear of "cool paddy fields, / wetlands slushy / with sweet mud," we hear the *neytal tiṇai*, "anxiety in love"; or when we hear of the river overflowing its banks and drenching the paddy, we hear *marutam tiṇai*, "the unfaithfulness of lovers."[2] Parakāla actually works very hard to name the specific flowers connected with the *caṅkam* landscapes—*kuriñci, neytal, mullai, marutam*—throughout his *tirumoḻis*.

Veṅkaṭeśa, though he knew this work, only hints at *caṅkam* motifs. His intent is not only to link himself to ancient tradition but also to creatively use it to preach to, to teach, and to debate with a contemporary audience of scholars (both rivals and allies), devotees, and poets fluent in both Tamil and Sanskrit. While doing this, of course, as I have argued here and in *Singing the Body of God*, he is eager to demonstrate his knowledge of Tamil tradition and mastery of the language. But the lyrical language of *caṅkam* Tamil is one of many forms used by Veṅkaṭeśa in his fundamentally didactic texts. There is, after all, as Friedhelm Hardy reminds us, a difference between an Āḻvār and an Ācārya.

If one carefully compares Veṅkaṭeśa's *kōvai* and "Garland" with Parakāla's *Periyatirumoḻi* III. 1–10, the similarities as well as the differences are striking in ways one might not expect. The two sets of poems follow similar overall patterns of "telescoping" description, beginning with the Lord of myth, the awesome and heroic forms of Vishnu,[3] and ending with the *arcāvatāra* and an evocation of place. Also, many of the same *avatāras* of Vishnu appear in each poet's praises. As we noted with the use of Devanāyaka's epithet, Veṅkaṭeśa obviously had his Āḻvār predecessor in mind when he composed his *prabandhams* to the same god.

Ultimately Veṅkaṭeśa's verses show a wider range of emotional and stylistic expression than do the *tirumoḻis*, which, with all their richness of imagistic detail, tend to be repetitive and predictable. Veṅkaṭeśa's poems do not simply repeat a pattern but rather trace the constant oscillation (themes with variations) between the poet's experience of divine majesty and accessibility, divine-human asymmetry, of cosmic presence and the emotional experience of absence. Parakāla's *tirumoḻis*, in comparison, are rather static, the mode being pure (and rather monotonous) praise.

But there are questions of genre here. This inner variety of style and feeling, this conscious inner polyphony, is indeed a reflection of Veṅkaṭeśa's creative use of the *prabandham* genre, a mixed-meter form that grants the poet more freedom to range metrically and thematically. And Parakāla, particularly in his uniquely powerful *maṭal* poems, is quite capable of invoking disruptive passions of love, intimacy, and radical asymmetry, and the mad oscillations of a lover whose beloved comes and goes at will, in ways that radically outstrip anything we read in Veṅkaṭeśa's theological visions.[4]

Perhaps in the end, the most striking difference between Parakāla, the Āḻvār of Tirumaṅkai, and Veṅkaṭeśa the Ācārya lies in the sectarian Ācārya Veṅkaṭeśa's more overtly didactic and theological purpose (and audience). His *prabandhams* are composed in a context of persuasion and debate, though they show an extraordinary depth and range of emotional experience and poetic skill.

But we should not take this last argument too far, either. There are deep links between Tirumaṅkaiyāḻvār and Veṅkaṭeśa on the level of institutional development. For this reason they are often linked by contemporary Vaṭakalai communities. It is significant that Tirumaṅkaiyāḻvār, unlike the other Āḻvārs, set out self-consciously to write a decad of verses *for every single sacred place* (*divyadeśa*) in Vaiṣṇava Tamil Nadu, and Tiruvahīndrapuram happens to be just one more stop on a long sacred itinerary. His poems, in ways quite similar to Veṅkaṭeśa's later work, are far from merely naïve lyric praises. They also map out a sacred itinerary at an important early stage of Śrīvaiṣṇava institutionalization. The two poets share a certain self-conscious awareness of what Hardy has called the "secondary structures" of a continually evolving Vaiṣṇava community and ideology.[5] In short, both saint-poets reflect, each in his own way, the growing institutionalization of the Śrīvaiṣṇava *sampradāya.*

Contrary to what the student of early Tamil *bhakti* poetry might expect, Veṅkaṭeśa's later, more cosmopolitan style of Tamil that seamlessly blends Sanskrit-influenced forms, vocabulary, and narrative strategies with the creatively transplanted voices of the Āḻvārs and classical Tamil *akam*, does not mute or overly "intellectualize" the emotional power of devotion. Rather, this later style adds to rather than diminishes the registers of religious emotion and experience in the devotional literature of south India.

I trust that both the similarities and differences between these two poets, so distant in time and milieux, will be instructive, and perhaps serve to shed further light on Veṅkaṭeśa's contribution to Tamil *bhakti* poetry. It will be obvious from the examples cited in this anthology that Tamil *bhakti* piety did not end with the age of the Āḻvārs.

Periyatirumoḻi III. 1–10 of Parakāla, Tirumaṅkaiyāḻvār

1

As the boar he squeezed between his cheek
  and one twisted tusk the broad cool earth;
he who slept in the cool deep black sea
  dwells here
    in Tiruvahīndrapuram
where footpaths lined with the fresh gold of pear blossoms[6]
  wind through groves
loud with bees that,
  tasting the nectar of lotus flowers,
sing sweet songs.

2

He holds in his lovely hand the glittering Discus;
  he offers half of his chest
  to the golden lady.[7]

Highest Lord who became the many meanings
  of the four
    chanted Vedas
  lives here,[8]

in Tiruvahīndrapuram,
loud with the sweet humming sounds of bees[9]
  in lotus flowers
  that loosen the knots of their petals
      when the female bees come,

in arbors on the mountain slopes woven
  of white *mātavi* blossoms.[10]

3

After he ate all seven worlds, Māyavaṉ,
  inscrutable god, stretched out
  on a banyan leaf:

                    Devanāyaka,
Lord of Gods who gives his body and his truth

to his servants,[11]

lives here,
in Tiruvahīndrapuram

that shines[12] with fertile wetlands red waterlilies[13]
and lovely swaying jasmine creepers[14]
that hug the fragrant champak
and *mātavi*[15]
thronging the slopes of the mountain
dark as his body.

4

Splitting into two the chest of the powerful demon
who dared oppose him, wild with anger,
he gave sweetest mercy to the child;[16]

this is his place,
Tiruvahīndrapuram,

shining in its loveliness[17] of cool paddy fields,
wetlands slushy with sweet mud,[18]
where the shade of sugarcane groves
is dark as sapphire[19]

and the tender young stalks, in dizzying array,[20]
swelling with juices,

are pressed down to earth

by the rim
of the sky.

5

After spanning with three strides this whole universe
at the horse sacrifice of great king Bali,
he fought the best of bulls
for that cowherd girl
slender
as a flowering
creeper;

he lives here,
in Tiruvahīndrapuram
tawny with golden blossoms[21]

where they eat cool jackfruit mixed with wild honey[22]
while troops of screeching monkeys

run and swing
in the branches
of kino

red cottonwood
and
champak.[23]

6

He who is the lovely color of a black rain cloud
wandering in the desert waste with that girl, slender as a creeper,
after the harsh words of the hunchback servant:

this radiant place
is his,
Tiruvahīndrapuram,

entwined with fertile groves where honey bees
wander, girt on all sides
by great rampart walls high as mountains on whose tops
the moon crawls
in its airy wanderings.[24]

7

That young prince who crushed the long heads of the island king
on the mountain cliff for that coy artless girl,
lithe as a creeper,
her waist
slender as lightning:

he lives here,
in cool
Tiruvahīndrapuram,

fanned by herds of great yak, full of tawny ripe paddy
where the gander sweetly rests with his geese

near beds of the big-petaled lotus flowers
in the shade of the mountain
dark
as sapphire.[25]

8

After he broke the bow for the sake of that girl whose soft black hair
gives off the fragrance of sweet musk[26]
he lifted the mountain like a royal parasol when the cows
ran scared
in the pounding rain:

he walks in this place,

Tiruvahīndrapuram,

bristling with holy tanks and ponds,[27] shining with its glittering
belt of the Eastern Ghats[28]

where the river,
overflowing its banks in surging waves
drenches the paddy fields;[29]
where fragrant eaglewood[30]
and the tusks of elephants in rut
are abundant
on the mountain.

9

Our great father who took in his hands the whip,[31]
driving the jeweled chariot for victorious Arjuna
in the brutal war of kings
who took up lances:[32]

this place is his,
Tiruvahīndrapuram

of cool stately mountain slopes
where the fertile river
flows into the paddy,
foaming with leaping fish;

where mountainsides are fragrant with tender young spathes
of areca palm
and creepers

lift
their tendril hands
bristling
with new shoots.

10

Sing these ten verses of cool metrical Tamil[33]
composed by lance-bearing Kalikaṉṟi
that elegantly speak of that delectable light[34]
in Tiruvahīndrapuram

where gods and demons,
again and again,
each in their own way,

worship he who swallowed
spat out
and measured the three worlds—

the one god become three—

and your sins
will vanish.

Notes

CHAPTER I

1. See Rebecca Manring, *Reconstructing Tradition: Advaita Ācārya and Gauḍīya Vaiśṇavism at the Cusp of the Twentieth Century* (New York: Columbia University Press, 2005), 17–43, for a detailed discussion of the uses of hagiography to understand the internal historical and theological development of a tradition, in this case, the Gauḍīya Vaiṣṇava tradition through narratives of the holy life of sixteenth-century sectarian teacher Advaita Ācārya. Manring is also preparing a volume of translations from the Middle Bengali *Advaita Prakāśa*, hagiographical narratives about Advaita Ācārya.

2. For a detailed treatment of narrative sources in the life of Veṅkaṭeśa, see my full-length study of the poet-philosopher, *Singing the Body of God*, 48–75. See also Satyavrata Singh, *Vedānta Deśika*, and Friedhelm Hardy, "The Philosopher as Poet—A Study of Vedāntadeśika's *Dehalīśastuti*." For a reference to the few historical/epigraphical sources we have of the poet's dates, provenance, and possible religiopolitical affiliations with Telugu kings and princes, see Filliozat's introduction to his translation of Veṅkaṭeśa's *Varadarājapañcāśat*. I quote in full a passage on Veṅkaṭeśa and the Telugu prince, cited at the beginning of this introduction: "A tradition recorded by Śrīnivāsasūri in his *Ratnapeṭika*, a commentary on [Veṅkaṭeśa's] *Subhāṣitanīvī* says that the king Śiṅga in Rājamahendra (Rajamundry), a distant disciple, by a desire to learn the tenets of Śrīvaiṣṇavas, sent śrīvaiṣṇava [sic] Brahmins to Vedānta Deśika in Śrīraṅgam, who received them and wrote for their king *Rahasyasaṃdeśa*, *Tattvasaṃdeśa* and one verse. This king can be identified with Siṅgaya Nāyaka who belonged to a royal family ruling at Koṛukuṇḍa (Rajamundry taluk) in the 14th century. The connection of

this family with śrīvaiṣṇava [sic] teachers is also known by other inscriptional sources. Siṅgaya Nāyaka appears in an inscription in 1368." The other source is the Śrīraṅgam inscription, treated in some detail in *Singing the Body of God*, and the colophon of a Telugu *kāvya*. See *Vedāntadeśika's Varadarājapañcāśat, with Sanskrit Commentary by Karūr Śrīnivāsācarya*, x.

3. See, for an exhaustive treatment of *anubhava* as devotional and ritual "experience," but even more as gestural commentary and "exegesis," see Archana Venkatesan, "Āṇṭāḷ and Her Magic Mirror: Her Life as a Poet in the Guises of the Goddess. The Exegetical Strategies of Tamil Śrīvaiṣṇavas in the Apotheosis of Āṇṭāḷ." (Ph.D. dissertation, Department of South and Southeast Asian Studies, University of California, Berkeley, Fall 2004). For a brief but important treatment of *anubhava* as performance, as acts of devotion, mimesis, and memory, see Davesh Soneji, "Performing Satyabhāmā: Text, Context, Memory, and Mimesis in Telugu-Speaking South India" (Ph.D. dissertation, Faculty of Religious Studies, McGill University, Montreal, April 2004).

4. From Veṅkaṭeśa's *Varadarājapañcāśat*, 45–47. Text taken from *Śrīdeśikastotramālā*, by Śrī Rāmatēcikācāryar. See discussion in *Singing the Body of God*, 193–194.

5. See Davis, *Lives of Indian Images*. I utilize the theoretical perspectives of Davis, along with the work of David Freedberg, C. F. Fuller, and Gérard Colas, among others, in my discussion of Veṅkaṭeśa's poems for icons in *Singing the Body of God*.

6. There is an intriguing functional equivalent to such a structure of asymmetry in the work of the great fourth-century CE. Eastern Orthodox Christian mystical theologian from Cappodocia, Gregory of Nyssa. In Gregory's *Dialogue on the Soul and the Resurrection*, and also in his vivid and elegant *Vitae* of his sister Macrina, such asymmetry of lover and beloved is represented, on the one hand, by "Gregory" himself as the weepy, emotionally vulnerable and needy lover, and on the other, his sister Macrina, as the ideal body of the saint, the *telos* of Christian experience, "dry" and impassible, whose transcendent *erōs* is channeled upward to god. I link these texts of Gregory to forms of "extravagant beholding" in the sequential bodily descriptions (*wasf; awṣāf*) of the Hebrew *Song of Songs* and Arabic *nasīb-ghazals*, and in Veṅkaṭeśa's Śrīvaiṣṇava *anubhavas*, in a forthcoming comparative study of love, ideal bodies, and particularity. For a relevant discussion of Gregory, see Virginia Burrus, "A Son's Legacy: Gregory of Nyssa," in *"Begotten Not Made": Conceiving Manhood in Late Antiquity* (Stanford: Standford University Press, 2000), 80–133. See also my article "Extravagant Beholding: Love, Ideal Bodies and Particularity."

7. See, among Panikkar's various articles and books that deal with this theme of the "tempiternal present," "El presente tempiterno." I also treat the theme of a transfigured time (and space) in the literary structure of Sanskrit poetry in "Lovers, Messengers, and Beloved Landscapes."

8. For a more detailed introduction to Veṅkaṭeśa as philosopher and poet, along with the significance of the themes of shrines, icons, and religious cosmopolitanism, see *Singing the Body of God*, 6–12.

9. See also *Singing the Body of God*, 80–82.

10. See his "Afterword" in *Hymns for the Drowning*, 103.

11. See Hardy, *Viraha-bhakti*, 241–280 and passim for an exhaustive literary, stylistic and structural analysis of the Āḻvār corpus of poems, the *Diviyapirapantam* (Skt: *Divyaprabandham*). The corpus itself, though it contained poems whose dates span the period between the sixth and ninth centuries, was itself compiled by the Ācārya Nāthamuni in the tenth century.

12. "Devotion" in the widest sense of the term would include Buddhist ritual veneration of images, texts, stūpas, and relics as well as Jain veneration of texts, Tīrthaṅkaras, goddesses (*yakṣiṇīs*), and teachers (*guru vandana*).

13. Any dating of the *Gītā* is by necessity only tentative. Van Buitenen dates its composition in circa 200 BCE. See *The Bhagavadgītā in the Mahābhārata*, translated and edited by J.A.B. van Buitenen (Chicago: University of Chicago Press, 1981), 6. For a discussion of the bhakti context of the *Harivaṃśa*, a post-*Mahābhārata* chronicle about the Vṛṣṇis and Andhakas that focuses on the Krishna legend, and early Purāṇas such as the *Viṣṇu* and *Brahma Purāṇas*, and Bhāsa's *Bālacarita-nāṭaka*, see Hardy, *Viraha-bhakti*, 65–104. For an excellent overview of theories on the development of various forms of bhakti, from Birardeau's global theory of bhakti that sees continuity from the Vedic *Yajur Veda*, Upaniṣads such as the *Kaṭha* and *Śvetāśvatara*, and the *Gītā*, to later forms of devotion, to those more recent approaches that emphasize localization that focus on "emotionalism," see Prentiss, *The Embodiment of Bhakti*, esp. the Introduction and 17–41.

14. See Stein, *Peasant, State, and Society in Medieval South India*, 78.

15. It is not entirely clear who these nonpeasant adversaries of the peasants of the Cormandel plain actually were. They are variously called by the name *kaḻabhra* (Pali: *kalabba*) or *kaḷavar*. Stein summarizes: "When, for how long, by whom and which of the Coromandel peasantry were subjugated is not clear. Whether it was a single conquering people from beyond the Tamil plain, as has been suggested, or from within the region, and whether the conquest was that of a single people or many, are queries unanswerable from the extant evidence" (ibid., 76–77).

16. Ibid., 78.

17. Ibid., 78–79. Stein quotes as sources for his remarks on Hsüang-tsang and inscriptional evidence on the ascendancy of "heretical" groups: K. A. Nilakanta Sastri, *The Culture and History of the Tamils* (Calcutta: Firma K. L. Mukhopadhyay, 1965), 113–114, and C. Minakshi, *Administraion and Social Life under the Pallavas* (Madras: University of Madras, 1938), 213–238.

18. For background on the period just before and after the ascendancy of Śaiva and Vaiṣṇava sectarian movements, see Leslie Orr, "Jain and Hindu 'Religious Women' in Early Medieval Tamil Nadu." Orr's richly documented discussion of Jain and Hindu women during this period belies any sense that Jains were either "foreigners" in the Tamil land, or somehow—as a persistent Hindu narrative would have it—"pessimistic, antisocial, anti-woman, puritanical, and un-Tamil" (187). For an attempt to reconstruct the lineaments of Tamil Buddhism during this period through a close reading of texts such as the *Maṇimēkalai*; one of the surviving Tamil Buddhist grammars, the *Vīracōḻiyam*, and its commentary; various commentaries on *caṅkam*

poetry; and a Tamil "translation" of Daṇḍin, see Ann E. Monius, *Imagining a Place for Buddhism.*

19. Stein, *Peasant, State, and Society in Medieval South India,* 80–81.

20. The Jains, according to the *Periyapurāṇam* account, lost two wagers with Campantar after the child saint had successfully cured the Pāṇḍiyaṉ of his sickness by singing a decad of praises to Śiva. One had to do with a test of fire, and another of water. In the first test, Campantar's verses inscribed on palm leaves survived a fire intact, while the inscribed leaves of the Jains burned to ashes; in the second test, yet another decad of Campantar's verses successfully drifted upstream against the powerful currents of the Vaikai River, while the Jains' inscribed leaves were hopelessly washed downstream. It is after these two losses that the Jains were impaled. For an English summary of this episode, see *Periya Puranam: A Tamil Classic on the Great Saiva Saints of South India by Sekkizhaar,* Condensed English Version by G. Vanmikanathan (Madras: Sri Ramakrishna Math, 1985), 245–262. There is also a striking fresco panel (ca. sixteenth-century Nayak) depicting the bonfire of the palm leaves, the river, and the impaled Jain monks on the outer walls of the Bṛhadīśvara temple in Tanjore. Whatever the veracity of this episode (it is Śaiva and Cōḻa in origin, and does not appear in Jain sources), it is a powerful index of the vehemence of this steady "shift" in power. See Chakravarti, *Jaina Literature in Tamil,* 31. For a detailed treatment of Tamil Śaiva constructions of Jains from the twelfth century, see Peterson, "Śramaṇas against the Tamil Way." See also Davis, "The Story of the Disappearing Jains," 213–224, and Prentiss, *The Embodiment of Bhakti,* 61–76.

21. For a nuanced treatment of Parakāla's hagiographical sources, see Hardy, "The Śrīvaiṣṇava Hagiography of Parakāla." For the general context, see Dehejia, "The Persistence of Buddhism in Tamil Nadu," esp. 58. See also, along with Parakāla's hagiography and the end-verses in his own poetry, the poems of Tirumaḻicaiyāḻvār (who is said to have been a Jain before his conversion to Vaiṣṇavism), and those of Toṇṭaraṭippoṭiyāḻvār for attacks and invectives against the Jains and Buddhists.

22. See Hardy, *Viraha-bhakti,* 242: "About ninety-five temples provide the external structure for this bhakti, and one could in fact define the 'movement' as the totality of Kṛṣṇaite bhakti culture associated with the ninety-five temples, from about the sixth to about the tenth century." For a discussion of the geography and chronology of the religious environments of the Āḻvār corpus, see ibid., 256–270. For a fine survey of the development of Śaiva self-identity from the Pallava period to the consolidation of the community with the *Periya Purāṇam,* see Prentiss, *The Embodiment of Bhakti,* 81ff. For an excellent treatment of pilgrimage in the Śaiva tradition and its role in the development of the poetry, see Peterson, "Singing of a Place." See also Gros and Gopal Iyer, *Tēvāram: Hymns śaïvites du pays tamoul,* lvii–lxi. For a thematic anthology of the Śaiva saint-poets, see Peterson's *Poems to Śiva.* For an overview of the Vaiṣṇava Āḻvārs and their sacred geography, see Ramanujan's "Afterword" to *Hymns for the Drowning,* and Hardy, *Viraha-bhakti,* 241–480. See also Cutler's study of both Śaiva and Vaiṣṇava materials in *Songs of Experience.*

23. In the case of the Vaiṣṇava *Divyaprabandham,* Hardy (*Viraha-bhakti,* 270–271) finds three different groups of poems: 1) reflective poetry in the *veṇpā* meter, each

stanza being linked to the previous one by *antāti*, i.e., where the last word of each stanza is repeated as the first word in the next, etc. This form has exacting rules of rhyme, assonance, and so on; 2) the "emotional song-poem" or *tirumoḻi*—a "sacred word-of-mouth"—what we might call "hymn"; each *tirumoḻi* contains nine or ten stanzas and a *phalaśruti* or final verse describing the merit accrued by listening to or reading the song; and 3) "experimental poems" that appropriate the idioms and images of earlier Tamil classical love poetry of the *Caṅkam* period (first to third centuries C.E.). Most notable is the *Tiruviruttam* of Nammāḻvār which, in Hardy's words, "replaces the *veṇpā* metre by the *viruttam* in the *antāti* structure, while experimenting with *akattiṇai* themes." *Akattiṇai* refers to the *akam*-style love poems of classical Tamil, a model for Āḻvār religious poetry (see discussion, particularly of Veṅkaṭeśa's Tamil *prabandhams* for Devanāyaka in chapter 4 of *Singing the Body of God*, 115–118, and below, "A Necklace of Three Jewels for the Lord of Gods: The *Mumaṇikkōvai*").

24. See Gros and Iyer, *Tēvāram*, for a discussion of the place of Āgamic ritual and esoterism in the poems of the Nāyaṉmār. Dennis Hudson for many years traced the Pāñcarātra ritual and esoteric elements in the poetry of the Āḻvārs through his study of the eighth-century Vaikuṇṭha Perumāḷ temple in Kāñcī. See *The Body of God: An Emperor's Palace for Krishna in Eighth-Century Kanchipuram* (forthcoming).

25. Most of these poems form Hardy's third group of poems in the Āḻvār corpus, though these motifs also appear in the *tirumoḻis* as well (see note 23 above).

26. See Stein, *Peasant, State, and Society in Medieval South India*, 83.

27. For a discussion of the early Ācāryas and their Sanskrit bhakti poetics, see Narayanan, *The Way and Goal*, and Nayar, *Poetry as Theology*. See also Gonda, *Medieval Religious Literature in Sanskrit*, 256–257, for a very short account of the Śrīvaiṣṇava *stotra* tradition with no reference to Tamil models. On p. 241 Gonda does mention, in a general way, possible Āḻvār influences on a genre of Sanskrit descriptive poetry.

28. Nayar, *Poetry as Theology*.

29. See Hardy, "The Philosopher as Poet," 278–279.

30. See *Singing the Body of God*, chapter 1, esp. 30–38, for a detailed account of the development of this tradition.

31. This combines two of Sheldon Pollock's theses on the flourishing of the Sanskrit "cosmopolis" in South Asia up to 1100, and his theories of the "vernacular millennium" and the "cosmopolitan vernacular." I treat in some detail these theories as they apply to Veṅkaṭeśa's use of Tamil, Sanskrit, and Prākrit throughout *Singing the Body of God* (see esp. 10–11 and Conclusion, 233–234). For Pollock's seminal essays, see "The Cosmopolitan Vernacular," "India in the Vernacular Millenium," and "The Sanskrit Cosmopolis, 300–1300."

32. See *Singing the Body of God*, chapter 2: 48–75, for a detailed account of the historiographical and hagiographical sources of Veṅkaṭeśa's life.

33. See the introductory sections of *Singing the Body of God*, 3–6, for a full account of this richly evocative scene, and the significance of these three languages.

34. See ibid., 12–15.

35. See Jorge Luis Borges, "Pierre Menard, Author of the Quixote," in *Collected Fictions*, translated by Andrew Hurley (New York: Penguin, 1999), 88–95.

36. For a detailed discussion of ideas about translation of Veṅkaṭeśa's poetry, see *Singing the Body of God*, 15–21.

37. See *Proensa: An Anthology of Troubador Poetry*, translated by Paul Blackburn, xviii.

38. See Benjamin's seminal essay "The Task of the Translator," 69–82; for quotation, see p. 80. Cf. also Benjamin's early essay "On Language as Such and on the Language of Man," where all names are merely a reflection (*Abbild*) of the singular transcendental divine Word, and all human languages, "naming words" (*nennendes Wort*), are "translations," in various orders of accuracy and magnitude, of that Word of God. See also Introduction to Benjamin, *Reflections*, xxiii.

39. Benjamin, "The Task of the Translator," 76.

40. See Steiner, *After Babel*, 302: "But there can be no doubt that echo enriches, that it is more than shadow and inert simulacrum. We are back at the problem of the mirror which not only reflects but also generates light. The original text gains from the orders of diverse relationship and distance established between itself and the translations. The reciprocity is dialectic: new formats of significance are initiated by distance and by contiguity. Some translations edge us away from the canvas, others brings us close." See also his concept of "vitalizing responsions" in *Real Presences*, 17. Cf. also my discussion of Veṅkaṭeśa's "reflexivity" in *Singing the Body of God*, 242–243. For an excellent discussion of translation as an art that affirms the original while creating a new poem, art translated as art, see Willis Barnstone, *The Poetics of Translation*, esp: 88–107.

41. See Smith, "A Twice-Told Tale: The History of the History of Religions' History," in *Relating Religion*, 362–374: "Indeed, the cognitive power of any translation, model, map, generalization or redescription—as, for example, in the imagination of 'religion'—is, by this understanding, a result of its difference from the subject matter in question and not its congruence. This conclusion has, by and large, been resisted throughout the history of the history of religions. But this resistance has carried a price. Too much work by scholars of religion takes the form of a paraphrase, our style of ritual repetition, which is a particularly weak mode of translation, insufficiently different from its subject matter for purposes of thought" (372). See also Smith's introduction to *Relating Religion*, "When the Chips Are Down," 28–32.

42. See Smith, "Close Encounters of Diverse Kinds," in *Relating Religion*, 303–322.

43. See *Singing the Body of God*, 15–21, from which some of this discussion is adapted.

44. From *Śrī Vedānta Deśika's Stotras (with English Translation)* by Late Sriman S. S. Raghavan et al.

45. For an excellent discussion of Tamil prosody that also points to parallels in Sanskrit and Prākrit, see Hart, *The Poems of Ancient Tamil*, 197–210.

46. One of the most extraordinary examples of the marriage of meters in two different poetic languages—a seventeen-syllable unrhymed modern Greek and English unrhymed hexameters (with some variation)—is Kimon Friar's magnificent translation of Nikos Kazantzakis's *The Odyssey: A Modern Sequel* (New York: Simon &

Schuster, 1958). See especially the Introduction, xxvi–xxxvi, and "An Additional Note on Prosody," 814–817.

47. See Hank Heifetz's *The Origin of the Young God,* his translation, with introduction, of Kālidāsa's *Kumārasaṃbhava,* a seminal early Sanskrit *kāvya,* and one of Veṅkaṭeśa's models. For south Indian bhakti poetry, there is Ramanujan's anthology of Nammāḻvār's Tamil poems, *Hymns for the Drowning;* Indira Peterson's anthology of Tamil Śaiva poems from the *Tēvāram, Poems to Śiva;* David Shulman's vigorous translations of Śaiva saint-poet Cuntaramūrtti, *Songs of the Harsh Devotee,* and Ramanujan's *Speaking of Śiva,* from the Kannaḍa *vacanas.* See also George Hart and Hank Heifetz's translations from the twelfth-century Tamil poet Kambaṉ, *The Forest Book of the* Rāmāyaṇa *of Kambaṉ;* Heifetz and Narayana Rao's *For the Lord of Animals,* poems from the Telugu of Dhūrjati; and, for all three of the language traditions important to Veṅkaṭeśa, Martha Selby's *Grow Long, Blessed Night,* an elegantly translated anthology of love poems from Sanskrit, Tamil, and Māhārāṣṭrī Prākrit. Cf. also, for north Indian texts, Vinay Dharwadker's *Kabīr,* Dilip Chitre's *Tukaram,* Chase Twitchell and Tony Stewart's *Lover of God;* and for a model outside of Indian literary tradition, see Michael Sells's translations of Arabic *qaṣīdas* and the *nasīb-ghazals* of Sufi poet Ibn 'Arabī: *Desert Traces,* "Ibn 'Arabi's 'Gentle Now' " and *Stations of Desire.*

48. See Panikkar, with the collaboration of N. Shanta, M.A.R. Rogers, B. Baumer, and M. Bidoli, *The Vedic Experience: Mantramañjarī,* and Merwin and Masson, *The Peacock's Egg.*

CHAPTER 2

1. *aṭiyarpāl meyyai vaittu:* here *mey* can mean both "truth" and "body." Cf. Veṅkaṭeśa's epithet for Devanāyaka, *aṭiyavārkku meyyanē,* "Lord of Truth to His Servants," taken from Tirumaṅkaiyāḻvār.

2. *aruḷ,* a rich word: "mercy" "compassion" "grace" "favor," "benevolence." *Aruḷ* can also take on the meaning of "freely becoming present, close, alive," and can approach the sense of "possession," open "emergent presence." In a more metaphorical sense, *aruḷ* can imply a certain "liquifaction." See Handleman and Shulman, *Śiva in the Forest of Pines,* 40–41. Cf. also Veṅkaṭeśa's *Dayāśatakam,* a Sanskrit hymn on Viṣṇu's divine mercy (*dayā; anukampayā; kṛpā*), personified, as it is here, as the goddess Śrī.

3. An iconographic and mythic reference: the icon of Vishnu has a small image of the goddess Śrī/Lakṣmī on its chest.

4. *aṉpuṭaṉ niṉṉōṭu avataritaruḷi:* "love" here is *aṉpu,* a word with rich textures of meaning, at once erotic and parental, love that melts and mingles. For a vivid essay on the various meanings, interpersonal and literary, of *aṉpu,* from *bhakti* poetry to love in a south Indian Śaiva family, see Trawick, *Notes on Love in a Tamil Family.*

5. Cf. *Viṣṇu Purāṇa* I.9.140–148 for a list of the female forms of Mahālakṣmī for each male form of Viṣṇu.

6. *mummaṇikkōvai moḻi*: the "three-jeweled necklace [of] speech."

7. *aruḷ*: "grace" or "mercy," but again with a sense, implied in the translation, of liquifaction, melting, the free flow of juices.

8. *iṉ amutak kaṭalāki niṉṟa*: "who stood/dwelt, as an ocean of sweet nectar," a verbal form that evokes the image of a "standing icon" and the shrine as setting for the visionary devotional experience. The image also combines image of liquefaction, free flow, and containment: Vishnu's flow is controlled, channeled upward.

9. *āyntu eṭukkunkāl*: "[when we] examine, take up; weigh the evidence."

10. Śrī here is *Tiru* in Tamil. The line is admirably concise in the original, playing on the polysemy of the word *Tiru*, meaning both the proper name of the goddess and "adornment": *niṉ tiruttaṉakkum ni tiruvāki*, "[you] become the *tiru* (adornment) for your Tiru herself, that is, you are the adornment for she who adorns you. A wonderful linguistic way of emphasizing the theological truth of the inseparability of *śakti* (goddess/power) and *śaktimān* (possessor of goddess/power).

11. *antam il amuta āḻiyāy niṟṟi*: see also previous verse 3.

12. *cīrk kaṇam cērnta cīlam ellai ilai*: *cīlam* [(Skt: *śīlam*)], which usually means morality, justice, righteousness, is glossed by the commentator here by *sauśīlam*, a Śrīvaiṣṇava technical term meaning "gracious condescension," implying divine accessibility.

13. *aruḷ*: "grace," "compassion," "benevolence."

14. The Tamil term *aṉaittum*, "all things," is glossed as *sakalatattuvaṅkaḷ*, all the *tattvas*. Veṅkaṭeśa uses a Tamil vocabulary to allude to the Pāñcarātra theology of the *tattvas* or "reals"—constituent, essential truths of reality. The seven *tattvas* of the Pāñcarātra are materially incarnated in various attributes of Vishnu's icon.

15. The original phrase possesses a lovely verbal music: *cittara maṇi eṉa tikaḻam maṉ uruvil.*

16. "[You] with the body [form] of the vast one who dwells in the sky," *viṇṇuḷ amarnta viyaṉ uruvataṉāl* (i.e., Vāsudeva). Throughout, Veṅkaṭeśa uses Tamil vocabulary for Pāñcarātra technical terms. My translation in this and the following verses sometimes glosses lines with some of the most important and familar terms, for the sake of clarity. The bilingual reader/listener would have immediately made the "translation," and perhaps would have relished the play of the two languages. *Vyūhas*: Tamil *urukkaḻ*, "forms."

17. *iṉ uru eṅkum eyti nī niṟṟi.*

18. A list of the *daśāvataras* or ten incarnations of Vishnu.

19. "sweetness": *iṉpam*, a vivid Tamil word meaning, along with a general sense of "sweetness," also joy, bliss, sexual pleasure.

20. "life-breath": *uyir*, most intimate "indweller," equivalent to the technical term *antaryāmin*, "indweller." "Bliss": *iṉpam*; also "sweetness," "joy."

21. *yāvarum aṟiyātu eṅkum nī karantu/ mēvu uruccūḻntu viyappinnāl mikuti.*

22. "Way/goal": Veṅkaṭeśa uses the Sanskrit word *gati*.

23. A thorny, theologically packed verse. Veṅkaṭeśa uses Tamil vocabulary, *vakai* (means, ways) and *paṭi* (forms) to "translate" the Pāñcarātra term *prakāra*: "modes."

24. *āṟum*: "way/path" [Skt: *upāya*].

25. Sanskrit "Dharma" here Tamil *aṟamum*.

26. *iṉpam*: literally, you are "sweetness," though as we have seen, this word is layered with devotional and erotic meaning.

27. *eṉatum nīyē*: literally, "you are *of* me" ("I am a part of you; I belong to you").

28. *iṉpam*: again, a rich word with connotation at once physical and spiritual: bliss, pleasure, happiness, love.

29. *niṉ uruniṉrum miṉ uru tōṉrum*: literally, "form appears [like] lightning from your standing/abiding form [icon]." A beautifully concise verse that expresses the poet's experience of the icon as cosmic-earthly-personal center of gravity, the universe in a single form, the whole in the part.

30. *aṉpu*: "tender," intimate love; affection, both parental and erotic, a term that gathers all the senses of "love" into one circle.

31. *uyyār*: they are not "living" (breathing) beings; they do not have life/breath.

32. Cutler, *Songs of Experience*, 82–83.

33. For reference to the *prabandham* genres, see Zvelebil, *Classical Tamil Prosody*, 44 and 91 passim. Cf. also Cutler on the *kōvai* and its bhakti uses, *Songs of Experience*, 82–83 passim. For an extended analysis of Veṅkaṭeśa's *prabandhams* and the "lost" Tamil lyrics, see *Singing the Body of God*, 116–118.

34. The theology of Vishnu and his mercy (*aruḷ*) summarized here is explored in great detail in Veṅkaṭeśa's Sanskrit *stotra Dayāśatakam* where the sacred hill, Tirumalai, is described as "the congealed form of Śrīnivāsa's mercy: / the streaming juice of the cane / become hard sugar candy" (*śrīnivāsānukampayā / ikṣusārasravantyeva yanmūrtyā śarkarāyitam //*).

35. This image alludes to a famous verse by an Āḻvār, Pokaiyāḷvār, from the first *Tiruvantāti* of the *Divyaprabandham* that describes the saint-poet laying "this garland of verses / at the feet of the Lord / who holds the dazzling wheel." For a discussion, see *Singing the Body of God*, 119, and Cutler, *Songs of Experience*, 123.

36. The story of Gajendra's rescue from the jaws of the crocodile (*gajendra-mokṣa*) has a long history in south Indian bhakti, from the *Bhāgavata Purāṇa* onward to the many vernacular literatures of devotion. See David Shulman's chapter on the Gajendra story in Potana's Telugu *Bhāgavatam*, "Remaking a Purāṇa."

37. For a more extensive commentary on this poem, see *Singing the Body of God*, 118–127.

CHAPTER 3

1. Shortened form of Tuvārakai, Tamilization of Dvāraka.

2. *nalium viṉaikaḷ cekum maruntiṉ nalam urainta verpinai*: a rich phrase and a common image in the Devanāyaka poems that identifies the god with the "medicine hill," holy ground and the god as healer (*marutiṉ*).

3. *vanai eṭuttu malai taṭuttu malaiyoṭu otta meyyiṉāṉ*: note the sonorousness and charming internal rhyme of the original verse phrase.

4. *aruḷ koṭuttu viṉai tavirkkum aṭiyavarkku meyyaṉē*: a theologically packed phrase, integrating the epithet, "he who is (body/truth) to his servants/slaves," with

his most common attributes, *aruḷ*, "grace," "mercy," fluid/open presence-power, and his power to destroy karma (*viṉai*).

5. "groves in the sand": *maṇal tōppil*, groves of casuarina that thrive in sandy soil, and are common along the Cormomandel coast.

6. *poruḷum aḻalum miṟaiyāka pūṇṭēṉ: aḻalum* is a rich word, meaning desire, lust, rage, also burning. I preserve both meanings here.

7. *añcaṇamum kāyāvum aṉaiya mēṉi: añcaṇa* is *kohl* or collyrium, a deep blue-black cosmetic used as makeup for the eyes. Its rich dark color is often used as a comparison for the dark color of Vishnu/Krishna's body.

8. "beauty of your body": *vaṭivu aḻaku.*

9. A string of beautiful images, also beloved by the Āḻvārs, and a lilting alliteration in the original Tamil: *maiyu[m] mā kaṭalum mayilum mā maṟaiyum maṇikaḷum kuvaḷaiyum koṇṭa meyyaṉē.*

10. *aṭiyōr meyyaṉē: mey* here, as noted elsewhere, means both "body" and "truth," so this epithet, usually translated Lord of Truth to His Servants or "Lord Who Is True to His Servants, implies both meanings. In the first line beginning "your holy body is dark," word *mey* is also used for "holy body" (*meyyaṉē*: he who possesses a body). This is a rather uncommon usage of *mey* as "body," but is used by Veṅkaṭeśa for euphonic reasons. I translate with this double usage in mind.

11. *mañcu ulāvu cōlai cūḻa ayintai*: "Ayintai encircled by groves which are overspread/enveloped by clouds."

12. *mācu il vācutēvaṉ*: "without flaw/taint Vāsudeva." The body of god is not merely material but is made of a "nonmaterial" matter (*śuddhasattva*). See Narayanan, "*Arcāvatāra*," 61–64.

13. *cem col*: "good" words, "straight" "true" speech. Initial rhyme with the *vem colāṉār*, the "hot" "cruel" "severe" speech of Yama's messengers, below.

14. Accuta: one who does not stumble or slip away; one who does not desert; indestructible; invincible: one of the "names" of Vishnu. Cf. Acyuta as the form of Vishnu who comes as a dam to prevent the destruction of Brahmā's sacrifice by Sarasvatī as a river in *Meyviratamāṉmiyam*, in *Singing the Body of God*, chapter 3: 79–114.

15. *mēvum aḻal matam: aḻal*: "heat," "rage," "fire," "anger," "lust." This is a very difficult, but theologically significant verse on radical surrender. I followed the commentator Rāmatēcikācāryar in attempting to construe it.

16. *poruttam poruntalum:* an ambiguous phrase: "concurring in agreement"; "agreement in what is fitting"; "in a way suitable [for each]."

17. *maṉ aṭaikkalam.*

18. *aruḷāl.*

19. *aṭi uraiyāl*: Sanskrit.

20. *cintaikavar pirākirutam.*

21. *ceḻuntamiḻ*: "rich, lovely, graceful, fertile"; Tamil.

22. Various game songs were adapted at an early period by religious poets to describe forms of divine love. Some of the best known of these devotional "game songs" were composed by Māṇikkavācakar. For a short study and translation of

Māṇikkavācakar's Tamil game songs, see Cutler, "Tamil Game Songs to Śiva," and *Songs of Experience*. See also the general study by Glenn E. Yocum, *Hymns to the Dancing Śiva*. Unfortunately all such works attributed to Veṅkaṭeśa are now lost. See discussion in *Singing the Body of God*, 117.

23. *muntai ma<u>r</u>ai mo<u>l</u>iya va<u>l</u>i mo<u>l</u>i nī e<u>n</u><u>r</u>u.*

24. See *Singing the Body of God*, 129.

25. See ibid., 127; and for a discussion of this pattern in Ā<u>l</u>vār poetry, Hardy, *Viraha-bhakti*, 330–331.

26. See Ramanujan, *Hymns for the Drowning*, 87–88, for reference to this *bhakti* theme of the "great in the little" in Nammā<u>l</u>vār.

27. This seems to imply that *mokṣa*, liberation, is granted to those who merely "see" and "remember" the *arcāvatāra* of Vishnu—a radical theology implied by Veṅkaṭeśa's poetry, but tempered by his prose. For a detailed discussion of Veṅkaṭeśa the philosopher and poet, see "Conclusion," *Singing the Body of God*, 232–243; for a more detailed thematic discussion of selected stanzas of the *Navamaṇimālai*, see ibid., 127–133.

28. I do also argue, in my larger study, for Veṅkaṭeśa's acknowledgment, somewhat against his theology of the necessity for a divine "pretext" (*vyāja*) in salvation, of divine love "without pretext" (*avyājavatsalya*) and the "unworthiness" (*akiñcanatvam*) of the devotee in certain passages of his poetry. There is a tension at times between Veṅkaṭeśa the poet and Veṅkaṭeśa the philosopher. See *Singing the Body of God*, 86–89; and also Hardy, "The Philosopher as Poet," for a similar argument in his reading of Veṅkaṭeśa's *Dehalīśastuti*.

CHAPTER 4

1. coral tree: the *mandāra* is one of five trees that grow in heaven. The original has a delightful lilting quality, particularly in its use of alliteration (repetition of *pa* sounds): *praṇatasurakirīṭa prānta mandāramālā / vigaḷitamakaranda snigdha pādāravindaḥ / paśupatividhipūjyaḥ padmapatrāyatākṣaḥ / phaṇipatipuranāthaḥ pātu māṃ devanāthaḥ.*

2. *praṇata*: bow, prostrate. The first word of the verse of the *stotra*. The last word of the last verse is *satyavadī*. When combined, these words make the phrase "Lord of Truth to those who bow down [to the Lord]"—according to commentators, an encryption of the Tamil epithet *aṭiyavarkku meyanē*, first used by Tirumaṅkaiyā<u>l</u>vār, and subsequently by Veṅkaṭeśa in his Tamil *prabandhams* to Devanāyaka.

3. *pūrvam*: "previous" in time, the early, the first, beginning. If this legacy were a body, this beginning would be the foot, root, etc., with the Ā<u>l</u>vārs and early Ācāryas as the waist and Rāmānuja the crown/head.

4. This phrase in one long compound: *devādhināthakamalāpṛtaneśapūrvam.*

5. Nāthamuni: the traditional founder of the Śrīvaiṣṇava *sampradāya*, who is also credited with collecting the four thousand verses of the Ā<u>l</u>vārs into an anthology (the *Divyaprabandham*) and instituting their recitation in homes and temples—and Nammā<u>l</u>vār, the most important Ā<u>l</u>vār.

6. *divye dayājalanidhau*: *dayā*: mercy, compassion; Tamil *aruḷ*.

7. *prācaḥ kavīn*.

8. *prācetasaprabhṛtikān*.

9. *nigamasamitasūnṛtoktīn*; *sūnṛtaḥ*: "true, pleasant, sincere, auspicious."

10. Address to Hemābjanāyakī, consort of Devanāyaka.

11. *prasādam*: "favor, grace," holy mercy.

12. The original phrase has a lilting quality, charming to the ear: *pṛthukajalpitavanmaduktim*.

13. *nigamottamāṅgaiḥ*: "by the highest/most exalted limbs of the Veda."

14. *ajñātasīmakam*.

15. *samādhiniyatairapi*.

16. *sāmi dṛṣṭam*.

17. *dāseṣu satya iti dhāraya nāmadheyam*: in Tamil, the epithet *aṭiyavarkku meyyanē*.

18. *antarvatīm giram*: "pregnant speech/words/language."

19. *viśeṣavidām anindyām*.

20. *stavyaḥ stavapriya itīva tapodhanoktam/ stoteti ca tvadabhidhānam avandhyaya tvam*.

21. *dustyājagāḍabandham*.

22. *sūtrānubadgdhaśakunikramataḥ*.

23. *gambhīrapūrṇamadhuram mama dhīr bhavantam/ griṣme taṭākamiva śītam anupraviṣṭā* / In the second two padas of this verse all adjectives modifying water—*gambhīra* (deep), *pūrṇa* (full), *madhuram* (sweet), and *śīlam* (cool) can be used to describe either God (*bhavantam*, You) or tank/pool (*taṭākam*).

24. *vyaktim*: (radiant) forms; appearances, manifestations.

25. Sun's circle: *savitṛmaṇḍalamadhyabhāge*.

26. "Mind/heart" of good people: *svānte satām*.

27. Another name of Auṣadhādri: "Medicine Herb Hill" at Tiruvahīndrapuram.

28. *vṛjina*: "wickedness"; *durgati*: "misfortune."

29. *prakhyātamauṣadhagirim*.

30. Bhagavān is a very important epithet of Vishnu as well as the Buddha in literary and inscriptional sources.

31. *svādhīna-viśva-vibhavam bhagavan*.

32. *viśeṣāt*, indeclinable, modifying the verb: call you "especially," "above all."

33. A very roundabout way of expressing this insight, which to commentators indicates the rhetorical trope of *ullekha*: a description of an object according to the different impressions caused by its appearance; *prāyaḥ*: "likely," "perhaps," "in all probability," modifying the verb *pratīmaḥ*: "we must admit that it is likely; we acknowledge."

34. *ahipurandaradhāmanātha*: "Lord of the fortress city of the king of serpents:" one of many versions of this epithet.

35. *sitāsitāni*: "luminous/pure/pale" and "nonluminous"; self-refulgent and non-self-refulgent.

36. *trayyantavṛddhagaṇināni*.

37. *cidacitpravibhāgavanti.*

38. *tava vigrahe' smin.*

39. *pratyaṅgapūrṇasuṣamāsubhagam vapuste.*

40. *priyābhir animeṣavilocanābiḥ.*

41. *nirjarapate*: a rather unusual form of the epithet.

42. *vedeṣu . . . nikhileṣu adhītam*: a rich phrase: which is "read in," "studied by," "declared by," even "understood by" or "taught by" all the Vedas.

43. *vibho*: the second vocative of the verse.

44. *viśvam.*

45. *kirīṭaḥ.*

46. *ekīkṛtadyumaṇibimbasahasradīptiḥ.*

47. *śarvarī*: "night," "twilight," from variegated, spotted. The image here is of a starry night, of night "spotted" with lights juxtaposed with the equally strong and pure light of a full moon. The visual experience of the Lord's body is expressed in a luxuriant coexistence of opposing images, both within and between stanzas (cf. the "thousand suns" image in the stanza above).

48. This phrase, combined with *śarvaryasau*, "this night," is highly alliterative: *kuṭilakuntaḷakāntirūpā*: "which has the form of shining/lovely curly locks of hair." I try to preserve some of the alliteration in other ways.

49. *samādhiyogyā.*

50. *laḷitakuṇḍaladarśanīyam . . . kanakakaitakakarṇapūram.*

51. "mark of grace": *lakṣmīḥ*: loveliness, [auspicious] grace, charm, splendor, beauty—also, of course, the goddess-spouse of Vishnu, eternally present on his chest.

52. *labdhā tithau kvacidiyam rajanīkareṇa.* This is the special phase/digit (*tithiḥ*) of *aṣṭamī*, half-dark/half-bright. "Moon" here is *rajanīkarī*, "night-maker," lending extra resonance to the word picture. See also Veṅkaṭeśa's *Paramapada Sopānam* for a simplar description of the brow.

53. *svedabindukaṇikodgatabudbhudāntaḥ*: literally, "the bubble of a particle of a sweat drop."

54. The *ūrdhvapuṇḍra* or the vertical chevron-shaped Śrīvaiṣṇava sectarian mark placed on the forehead.

55. The original pada skillfully combines *l*-sounds with palatal and dental *t*-s that call to mind the onomatopaeic *taṭataṭa* for rumbling or thunder.

56. *śrutim*: "hearing," "ear." The plural is less awkward in English.

57. *āśāgaṇaprasavahetum*: "cause of the creation of the groups of directions." The obvious source of this is the Puruṣa Sūkta, *Ṛg Veda* X. 90.

58. Used twice, *āśāḥ* means both "directions" and "desires."

59. Phrase culled from the epithet of Kāma used here—*kandarpa*—of doubtful etymology, but often seen to be from *kaṃ-darpa*, "inflamer even of a god." See Monier-Williams, sv.

60. *puṣyati . . . vividhān vihārān*: "displays many pleasures/games/enjoyments" (*līlaikaṇkaḷ*—*līlās*—in the Tamil glosses).

61. The verse is a *śleṣa*, an elaborate punning on fish and earring: Makarikā is from *makara*, fish or sea monster. Thus the phrase *pratimukhasthitidarśanīyā*,

modifying "the ornament Makarikā," can mean either "beautiful to behold [to those who] stand in front of you" (the context of temple darśan) or "beautiful to behold standing against/opposite your face"—here in the metpahorical sense of "swimming against the current." I try to preserve both meanings in my translation.

62. *nijam ādhirājyam.*

63. *akhilajantuvimohanārhā . . . mātṛkā . . . kāmaśarāsanasya*: "The model for the bow (arrow-shooter) of Kāma capable of making to swoon/deluding/bewildering all creatures." The erotic mood begins to take over at this point in the *anubhava*, and steadily grows in intensity.

64. *ālakṣyasattvam.*

65. *snigdhāyatam*: "glossy/tender/affectionate and long/extended." *Snigdhā* is a rich and common, and well-nigh untranslatable, word.

66. *prathimaśāli* can be taken to modify either the *vilocanam* (eye) or the *dugdhāmbudheḥ* (Milky Ocean).

67. *vaimānikādhipa.*

68. "miming": *viḍambita*, "to be like/to imitate."

69. This phrase attempts to translate the rich resonances of the rather terse phrase *anāmayavākyagarbhaiḥ*: "pregnant/holding in a womb words [about our] health/welfare."

70. *nabhaścarapate.*

71. "snorts": *niḥśvasitaḥ.*

72. *āśvāsinī bhavati saṃprati muhyate me*: a rich but concise phrase, translated here with an ear to the sound of the original (the nasals, breathy *bha*-sounds, and sibilants). Literally: "[the nose] soothes/comforts/revives/cools me who am faint/swooning."

73. *bimādharam spṛśati rāgavatī matirme*: "my mind/a passionate lady touches/kisses [your] *bimbā* lower lip." *Rāga*—passion—here also evokes the color red of the *bimbā* fruit and the *pārijāta* flower.

74. *āruṇyapallavitayauvanapārijātam*: *Pārijātam* is the coral tree, one of five trees of paradise; *bimbā* in Tamil is *kōvai paḻam*, often used by Nammāḻvār and other Āḻvārs to describe the color of the Lord's lip.

75. *vismerabhāvarucirā*: "lovely/radiant/beautiful because of the state of wonder/astonishment," modifies both the garland and the "mind" of the poet, taking on different nuances with each object. I have doubled the phrase in translation.

76. A remarkably lilting phrase, with internal rhyme: *padmālayāvalayadattasujātarekhe*, "with lovely marks/lines/traces made by the bangles of she who sits in the lotus."

77. This is a characteristically richly evocative phrase, one deeply but subtly erotic: *tvātkāntimecikasaṅkhanibhe*, "like the conch blue-blackened by your [dark] loveliness/[female]beauty/brightness, lovely color." I retain here the image of the dark eye of a peacock's tail evoked by the word *mecika* for its Krishna associations.

78. *dhīḥ* (mind) is an impossibly rich word whose connotations and importance go back to the *Ṛg Veda*: thought, meditation, devotion, prayer, understanding, intelligence, wisdom, poetic/visionary insight.

79. *jātasaṅgā*: fondly, deeply attached.

80. *tridaśapuṅgava*: *puṅgava* is bull, hero, chief, a martial image. An unusual version of the epithet, emphasizing the image of the warrior.

81. *alaṃkṛtahetijālaiḥ*.

82. A phrase that translates the compound *jitapārijātaiḥ*: "[the arms] by which *pārijāta* is won/vanquished." *Pārijāta* is one of the five trees of paradise, the coral tree.

83. *nīlācaloditanisākarabhāskarābhe*: "in a single instant" is added to the verse to emphasize the sense of *abhūtopama* or "impossible analogy" (i.e., the sun and moon can never rise at the same time).

84. *jagati svabhūmnā*, in the last pada, modifies the finite verbal phrase, "inspires confidence," though this phrase might also be taken to modify *śāntāhite* in the second pada, "silence [your] enemies."

85. *bhajatām*: to those "devoted ones," the *bhaktas*, those who love/enjoy [you]. Commentaries give *caraṇamaṭai bhavarkaḷukku*: "to those who have surrendered to/taken refuge in [you]."

86. *bhaktānurañjanam*: "delighting/inspiring affection/devotion in your *bhaktas*."

87. *nityāparādhacakite hṛdaye*.

88. *bāhumadhyam*: literally, "between the arms," the chest.

89. "Daubed with . . . designs," *patrabhaṅgam*: auspicious lines drawn on the face, hands, or other parts of the body with unguents or henna. Here wounds are turned into lovely drawings on the warrior's chest of the Lord.

90. *durdantadaitya*.

91. This is one long compound phrase in the original, with its own music: *śrīvatsa-kaustubha-ramā-vanamālikāṅkam*. "The mole with its curl of white hair, Śrīvatsa:" To refer to Śrīvatsa, the "mark" on Vishnu's chest as a "mole" is distinctive to south Indian descriptive particularity with regard to the body of god. This Śrīvatsa in the Tamil sources (the commentaries on the poems) is referred to as *maccam* or *maru*, even *Tirumaru*, which means "mole, wart, freckle; black spot;" *Tirumaru* would literally be sacred mole. This particular "mole"/mark, however, is luminous, and has a tuft of luminous hair. It takes on a more symbolic sense in later texts and icons, taking on a cruciform flower shape on the chest of Vishnu. But as a "mole" and/or whorl of hair, it is a vivid mark on the "flesh-body" of god. This kind of detail is quite characteristic of the concrete physical reality the body of Vishnu takes in the shrine poems, in the "devotional eye" of the poets and also of the commentators, a living, physical presence, however spiritualized (the icons are made, after all, of *śuddhasattva*, "pure matter"). The rather general dictionary sense of "mark" with hair, or merely a "hair tuft" or swirl/whorl of hair, is made more specific in the maṇipravāḷa and Tamil commentaries. This is the sense of *Devanayakapañcāśat* verse 32 and *Acyutaśatakam* 28 and 36.

92. *varṇakrameṇa*: *varṇa* literally means "color," though it also means "class" or "kind," bringing to mind again the *Ṛg Veda* Puruṣa Sūkta. "Attributes" is used here in the sense of something following a fixed set of characteristics, while "color" is used in the following line to translate the sense of *vicitra*, "many-colored."

93. *vicitritāṅgī*: its parti-/multicolored/variegated "limbs."

94. *smeraprasūnasubhagā*: *smera* can mean both "smiling" and "freshly blown," referring to the garland and the icon's face.

95. *ajahatkamalāmaṇindrā*: *ajahat* here has the literal sense of "not losing or dropping." Commentators gloss this word as *piriyātayāy*: "inseparable" [from Lakṣmī and Kaustubhā].

96. *nityā tava sphurati mūrtiriva dvitīyā.*

97. *āśritatārakam*: "uplifter of those who take shelter [in You]." Each descriptive compound can be taken at once to describe both moon and the Lord's mind. See discussion below.

98. *sumanasām amṛtam duhānam*: also "dispenser of immortality to good persons."

99. *samṛddhakāmam*: "by whom desires/passion is fulfilled."

100. *tat tādṛśam*: the Tamil commentators gloss this as *aṟputamāṉa*, "astonishing, wonderous."

101. *valitrayavibhāvyajagatvibhāgam.*

102. *āmoditanābhinalinasthaviriñcabhṛṅgam.*

103. *ārādhayadbhiriha tairbhavataḥ.*

104. *parivāravatī sujātā: sujātā* can either mean "well-made [belt]" or "well-born/high-born girl." The entire verse is a *śleṣa*, a complex pun where each descriptive phrase can apply to the waist belt (*raśanā*) or to a young woman in love. See discussion in *Singing the Body of God*, 210–211.

105. *pītambareṇa.*

106. *strīratnakāraṇam*: the nymph Ūrvaśī.

107. *yauvanagajendrakarābhirāmam*: "whose loveliness is [like] the trunk of a king of elephants who is youthful." I have extended the line in English to give a sense of the lilting quality of the original, along with its suggestive imagery.

108. *ūrīkaroti bhavadūruyugam mano me.*

109. *lāvaṇyapūralalito ūrdhvaparibhramābham.*

110. *gopāṅgaṇeṣu kṛtacaṅkramaṇam.*

111. *dūtye dukūlaharaṇe vrajasundarīṇām.*

112. daityas: demons or *asuras.*

113. *kandarpakāhalaniṣaṅgakalācikābham.* The epithet Kandarpa, according to some, means "inflamer even of gods."

114. *sāmānyadaivamuśanti padam tvadīyam.*

115. *anyābhilāṣaparilolam*: "tossed/shaken by desires [for] other [things]."

116. *āvarjitābhiḥ . . . nijāṃśujālaiḥ:* "incline toward one another by the accumulation of their own rays/[luminous] points/ends." Tamil commentators gloss this as *tamuṭaila oḷit tokutikaḷāl. Jālaḥ* here can also refer to "webs" or membranes between the toes of holy persons and divinities. In this sense, it is the luminous webs that draw the toes together.

117. I have here uncharacteristically reversed the word order of the original (which begins with a description of the toes), for the sake of clarity.

118. *tvadīyapadayor nakharatnapaṅktiḥ*: "the row of nail-jewels on your two feet."

119. This is one long melodious compound: *vajra-dhvaja-aṅkuśa-sudhā kalaśa-ātapatra-kalpadruma-amburuha-toraṇa-śaṅka-cakraiḥ . . . matsyādibhiḥ*.

120. *viṣvañci . . . vedhaḥsvahastalikhitāni durakṣarāṇi*: Brahmā's "ubiquitous" (*viṣvañci*) "headwriting."

121. *yogam vinā'pi*: "even without yoga"—here, the spiritual discipline of devotion, *bhakti yoga*—earned through many past lives.

122. *tvadīyapadapadmaparāgayogāt*.

123. *śuddhadharmāḥ*.

124. *tvajjīvitaiḥ*.

125. *durlabhaiḥ*.

126. *svayamātmavantam*.

127. *niṣkiñcanatvadhaninā:* "(by one whose) wealth/treasure is helplessness/having nothing/poverty."

128. *nānāvidhaprathitayogaviśeṣadhanyāḥ*: I have extended the phrase a bit, trying to catch the quiet irony and gentle pomposity of the original.

129. *śatakoṭitamāṃśakakṣyām*.

130. *ātmāpahārarasikena:* "[by me who is] a connoisseur of stealing (my) self/body/'ātman.'" I have translated in the active voice a passive construction in the original, for the sake of clarity. This is a very difficult verse to translate fluidly into English.

131. *dattam . . . anyairadhāryam*.

132. *akiṃcanasārvabhaumam*: "emperor of worthlessness." *Akiṃcana* is an important theological term here. See discussion in *Singing the Body of God*, 213–214.

133. *vibudhādhirāja*.

134. *vātyāśataiḥ viṣayarāgatayā vivṛttaiḥ / vyāghurṇamānamanasam*.

135. *nityopataptamapi mām [manasam] nijakarmadharmaiḥ*.

136. *nirveśaya svapadapadmamadhupravāham*.

137. *darśitābhīṣṭadānaḥ:* "(by whom) desired gifts are made manifest."

138. *gandhahastīva*.

139. *jaya*.

140. *ādyam*.

141. *narakamathanadakṣam*.

142. *vinataviṣayasatyam:* "the truth in respect to those who bow/bend [the knee]." I translate here also using the image of "body," alluding to Veṅkaṭeśa's Tamil epithet for Devanāyaka, *aṭiyavarkku meyyanē*: "he who is body/truth to his slaves/servants."

143. *stutipadam adhigacchan*: literally, "finding/obtaining" You (*tvām*) in "padas of stutis."

144. *śobhate satyavādī*: literally, shines as one whose "word is truth."

145. See chapter 14 on "Stotra Literature" in Gonda's *Medieval Religious Literature*, 232–233, 246–247, and passim.

146. See Panikkar, "El presente tempiterno."

147. For a detailed thematic summary of the *stotra*, which I will not reproduce here, see *Singing the Body of God*, chapter 7, "An Ornament for Jewels," 199–215.

148. See Kampaṉ, *Irāmāvatāram*, Pālakaṇṭam, Kolaṉkāṇ Patalam, 3 (the *kēcāti-pātam* of Śītā). There it is the jewels that cover the natural beauty of Sītā. See discussion by D. Ramaswamy Ayyangar in *Devanayaka Panchasat of Vedanta Desika*, 26–27. Ramaswamy Ayyangar also cites an Araiyār tradition at Śrīraṅgam of describing the Lord as "Perumāḷ who gives beauty to the adornments" (*āparaṇattukku aḻaku koṭikkum perumāḷ*). See, for a detailed study of the Araiyār liturgical tradition of Śrīraṅgam, Narayanan, *The Vernacular Veda*. See also *Singing the Body of God*, chapters 5 and 7, pp. 135–165 and 204–213.

149. See also *Varadarājapañcāśat* 48, in *Singing the Body of God*, chapter 6: 193–195. See, also, for similar images of passionate gazing among the works of Ācārya-poets, Yāmunācārya's *Stotra Ratna* 44 and Kūreśa's (Kūrattāḻvāṉ's) *Varadarāja Stava* 100 (where it is Lakṣmī who enjoys her Lord). See also the last verse of Appayya Dīkṣitar's *Varadarāja Stava*.

150. See my article of some years ago, "In Love with the Body of God," for reference to *anubhavas* and *wasfs* (stepwise descriptions of lovers' bodies) in the *Song of Songs*. I am currently working on a long-range comparative project on love, ideal bodies, and particularity that expands on this topic. See my article "Extravagant Beholding."

151. See Davis, *Lives of Indian Images*, 11, for a reference to the poet's "devotional eye."

152. For versions of the story of the icon of Vishnu as Raṅganātha and the Muslin princess, see ibid., 132–135. See also Vasudha Narayanan, "*Arcāvatāra*: On Earth as He Is in Heaven."

153. See Ramanujan, *Hymns for the Drowning*, 122–123.

CHAPTER 5

1. *Accuyam* (Skt: Acyuta), one of the three epithets here, means "He who does not stumble." One of the "names" of Vishnu in the *Viṣṇusahasranāma* (mentioned in 101, 319, 557, and in the *namāvalī*). The epithet has also been interpreted to mean "He who prevents [his devotees] from stumbling."

2. Veṅkaṭeśa's use here of the second person imperative *ṇamaha* (Skt: *namata*), "bow down to, worship, do homage to," is unique to this *stotra*. D. Ramaswamy Ayyangar, following a tradition of Śrīvaiṣṇava commentators, compares this second person request to the genre of request poems in the Āḻvār corpus, where the saint-poet, in the voice of the *nāyakī*, calls out to all creatures to praise the Lord (see *Acyuta Satakam of Vedanta Desika*, 4–5). There is little here to substantiate the immediate presence of a "love-sick" girl, though such a reading foregrounds the general tendency among the commentators to read the entire poem in the nuptial mode. Later, particularly by way of this same image of the elephant on the river banks, and in the long *anubhava*, we will see many erotic elements enter the texture of the poem. The shrine, the river, and its "Medicine Hill" at Tiruvahīndrapuram are here, as in the other poems to Devanāyaka, highly mythologizied and eroticized. Note that the Lord is described here as both a *tamāla* tree on the Garuḍa's banks (*gālulaṇaitaṭatamālaṃ*)

and as "steady radiance" (*thirajoim*). The *tamāla* tree conjurs an image of coolness and darkness, being a shade tree with broad green leaves and dark bark; "inextinguishable radiance," of course, is intense brightness. This is one of a string of images throughout the poem that emphasize what in verse 34 is called the Lord's "power to make the incoherent cohere."

3. Here begins a string of vivid, sometimes starkly drawn, deprecatory verses emphasizing the poet's inadequacy before his task of hymning Acyuta. "Sweet lisping tongue" is *saaṃbhugehiṇivilāsāhittamarī*. Devotional asymmetry is part of literary convention here.

4. "streaming moonlight": *kittijoṇhāpasare—kitti* (Skt: *kīrti*) can also mean "beauty"; "like ditchwater": *racchāsalilaṃ va—racchā* (Skt: *rathyā*) is a powerful counter-image of the majestic Gaṅgā.

5. As in the *Devanāyakapañcāśat*, Veṅkaṭeśa includes praise verses in honor of the Ācāryas, mediators on the path of *bhakti* and *prapatti*.

6. "murky hearts": *kasāyakaburesu* (Skt: *kaṣāyakabureṣu*) can mean spotted with filth or blotched with impurities.

7. *tivihantam* (Skt: *trividhāntam*): "threefold limitations": time, space, objects. Commentators interpret verses 8–25 as describing the *svarūpa* or "self-form" (the transcendental nature) of the Lord as articulated in the Upaniṣads, Brahma-sūtras, and Rāmānuja's commentary on the Brahma-sūtra, *Śrī Bhāśya*).

8. *paḍivatthupuṇṇo (prativastupūrṇaḥ)*... *apaḍihaaṇiaṭhiri (apratihatanijasthitiḥ)*: "surrounding/filling/pervading all things... you establish yourself unobstructed(ly)."

9. This verse is filled with Sanskrit technical terms from the Brahma-sūtra literature. *Puruṣa, pradhāna*: "soul/person," and "matter"; *upādānam*: "material cause"; *nimittatvam*: "efficient/instumental cause." "Creative will" is *saṅkalpa*; "inscrutable power" is *śakti*.

10. "manifest [material] power": *vihūī* (Skt: *vibhūti*); "your radiance": *sirī hoi* (Skt: *Śrīrbhavati*): Śrī is simply another name for Vishnu's consort-goddess Lakśmī, here characteristically seen as both other and as utterly part of the male, as the male's shining "brilliance" or "radiance." There are many ambivalent gender issues here. The entire universe is nothing more, nothing less, than Vishnu and Lakṣmī, or rather, all things are really nothing but the Lord, the singular *Brahman* of the Upaniṣads, as commentators on this verse note, citing passages in the *Vishnu Purāṇa* and *Śrī Bhāśya*.

11. *āṇattī tuha alaṅghaṇijjapahāvā*: your command is not "overstepped/overpowered/overmastered."

12. "death rituals": *śrāddha* rites. Brahman priests who are "consecrated by mantras"—Veṅkaṭeśa's phrase here is *ṇimantiabamhaṇa* (Skt: *nimantritabrāhmaṇa*, "mantrified")—stand in for the ancestors, and are fed in place of them. The real "enjoyers," however, of the *havis* or ritual offerings of the *śrāddha* are, of course, the ancestors themselves. In this same way, all Vedic rituals set down in the Vedic injunctions have for their ultimate/transcendental end (enjoyer) solely the Lord.

13. "nourishing mother-spirit": *pasūī* (Skt: *prasūtī*), "source"/"yielder"/literally, "mother/what brings to birth"; "showing no favor . . . the same": *samo khu* (Skt: *samaḥ khalu*): the phrase translates *samaḥ*, "sameness"/equanimity/impartiality.

14. *pesaṇam vi* (Skt: *preṣaṇamapī*): *pesaṇam* here has the meaning of messenger/servant/go-between. The immediate context would be Vishnu as Krishna, messenger between armies working for the Pāṇḍavas in the *Mahābhārata* war, but also other "services," such as charioteer, along with other examples of the Lord's "services."

15. This verse is filled with essential Śrīvaiṣṇava theological teaching about the Lord as the true *siddhopāya*, "perfected means" (of salvation), both "way" and "goal." The act we perform for the sake of the Lord's attention, so that he will grant us grace, is *sādhyopāya*; the object of this *sādhyopāya*, when he grants us our wish, is the *siddhopāya*. See note in Sri D. Ramaswamy Iyengar's edition of this poem, *Achyuta Satakam of Vedanta Desika*, 22–23. See also Narayanan, *The Way and the Goal*, 133 and note on 207.

16. Now begins the evocation of the *guṇas* or "auspicious attributes/qualities" of the Lord, following the descriptive verses above detailing the *para-svarūpa* of Devanāyaka.

17. "flame of dark sapphire": *sāmalamoho* (Skt: *śyāmalamayūkhaḥ*), "dark/blue-black flame."

18. "never having passed even into young manhood": *akumārajovvaṇathiam* (Skt: *akumārayauvanasthitam*); "sweet happy": *suham* (Skt: *sukham*).

19. This is both a description of the holy icon-body (*tirumēṉi*) in the temple shrine and the *svarūpa*, the "self-form" or "transcendental" (ethereal) form of Vishnu-Devanāyaka.

20. After an evocation of the many theological forms of Vishnu-Acyuta in verses 7–32, from the *para-svarūpa* form to the Upaniṣadic *antaryāmī* who "shines like a flame of dark sapphire in the hearts of sages" (verse 27), and the divine and auspicious supernal body of Vishnu with his consorts in heaven, we begin here a slow descent into the sanctum of the temple and a head-to-foot *anubhava* of the Lord. The landscape from now on takes on an unequivocally sensual texture.

21. Here is Vishnu-Devanāyaka as Gajendra again, the Lord of Elephants, on the banks of the river—but now taking on an image at once martial and erotic. See also *Devanāyakapañcāśat* 52, above.

22. "make the incoherent cohere": *aghaḍiyaghaḍaṇāsattiṃ* (Skt: *aghaṭitaghaṭanāśaktim*: literally, "who has the power bring together what is not together"); *aghaṭamāna* is "incoherence." Another possible translation might be "to hold the opposites in tension together." I am grateful for John Carman's helpful suggestions on this point.

23. Veṅkaṭeśa, like the Āḻvārs, delights in this image of the "big in the little." It aludes to Vishnu the baby the size of a banyan leaf who holds all the worlds in his belly, as well as to the episode of the baby Krishna opening his mouth and revealing to his foster-mother Yaśodā all the worlds inside of him. Here the poet is imagining this "big" universe in the little space of the icon's belly. See

Devanāyakapañcāśat 35, above. See also verse 5 of the *Bhagavaddhyānasopānam* in *Singing the Body of God*, chapter 5: 158–159.

24. The image here of "the yellow cloth streaked with red" (*paripāḍalambara*) refers both to the *pītāmbara* of the temple image and the mythic exploits of Lord Vishnu. The next verse (41) also follows this pattern.

25. See also *Bhagavaddhyānasopānam* 3, in *Singing the Body of God*, chapter 5: 158.

26. *amiyasāyurasam* (Skt: *amṛtasvādurasam*).

27. An extraordinarily vivid image of seeing as a kind of touching. *Darśana* here is analogous to applying *añjanam* (collyrium or *kohl*, lady's eye-black) to the eyes, an image that conjures up coolness and a glossy darkness often associated with the sanctum icon of Vishnu, as well as the erotic image of the Lord as makeup for a woman's eyes. See in this context the Bengali poem (ca. 15th–16th century) by Vidyāpati that describes Krishna as "*kohl* to the eyes" of the beloved, in *In Praise of Krishna*, translated by Dimock and Levertov, 15. The *añjanam* here is a *siddhañjanam*, the eye-black of *siddhas*, tantric ascetic healers. This is a kind of magic eye-black that is thought to have visionary powers, as well as the powers to find hidden treasures. *Siddhañjanam* can also mean "perfect or perfected" *añjanam*. I follow the commentators here in emphasizing the image of the *siddha* tantrics, particularly because of the reference to finding "the hidden treasure" of Lakṣmī.

28. Thus ends the formal *anubhava*. Whereas the previous verse 45 emphasized seeing, this one puts the emphasis on "being seen," both components of *darśana*. Now begins a praise of devotees, those who surrender to Devanāyaka at his powerful shrine. Along with the praise of devotees, there runs, alongside as a double current, the praise of the powers of the shrine as a "heaven on earth."

29. *jīvantamukkasarisā*: these *bhattā* (Skt: *bhaktāḥ*) live as though they already were *jīvantamukka*, liberated in this body. Here the qualifier *sarisā* (Skt: *sadṛśā*), "as if," is theologically very important. Veṅkaṭeśa argued strenuously against the concept of the *jīvanmukta* in his philosophical and polemical prose writings—but here, as in all his poetry, we find the boundaries a bit blurred. As we have seen, his poetic praises of the extraordinary powers of the shrine and of its icon stress their powers to grant liberation here, on this earth, to those who surrender. Veṅkaṭeśa the poet here follows Veṅkaṭeśa the philosopher.

30. A lovely image, in the poem the alliterative compound *ghanakandaḷi-kandakayaḷi-khambhasamāyim* (Skt: *ghanakandaḷi-kandakadaḷī-stambhasamāni*), "like [soft] stems of the plantain [and] roots of thick *kandalī*." I add, in my translation, the "image in the word": for after the rains, especially in the monsoon season, white blossoms of the *kandalī* plant, notorious for its frail roots, appear in thick clusters, then soon disappear. Both examples, of course, are images of frailty and transience.

31. The phrases, modifying *dosā* (stain/fault), "children of infatuation" and "born of delusion," are both taken, with some freedom, from the original phrase *mohasuā dosā* (Skt: *mohasutā doṣā*).

32. Another allusion to a universe transfigured and renewed—in the here and now—in the presence of the *arcāvatāra*. The devotee at the shrine lives, at this very moment, "the end of history."

33. It is noted by commentators that Veṅkaṭeśa refers here to the ideas that a dying person will see two moons and also a hole in the disc of the sun. See note in Ramaswamy Iyengar, *Acyuta Satakam*, 45–46.

34. An image, common in Veṅkaṭeśa, of religious ecstasy in the midst of *darśana* and *pūjā*. See also the curious *śleṣa* of *Devanāyakapañcāśat* 37, above.

35. This sentiment becomes very important in understanding the centrality of the shrine and its icon-body: true devotees will not, ultimately, desire liberation at all, but rather rebirth *here*, so that they might always be near the Lord on earth in the "beloved landscape" of the temple, where the presence of god is more available than in heaven. "Hold fast to their bodies," literally, "hold to their senses" (*karaṇāi*); exist, remain.

36. A critical, if subtle, point of doctrine. Though normally Veṅkaṭeśa will emphasize, in his theological and scholastic writings, that the formal preparations of the *bhaktimarga*, such as ritual prestations, fasts, prayers, and meditations, are necessary pretexts (*vyāja*) for grace and salvation, in his poetry he emphasizes, as here, simple surrender (*saraṇam*), without any "pretext," as the only way to salvation (*muttā*). His poems argue for a theological position that approaches that of his scholastic opponents, the Ācāryas of the southern (Teṉkalai) school. For a detailed discussion of this, see Hardy, "The Philosopher as Poet," and *Singing the Body of God*, 175–180, 190, 235–236.

37. This verse expresses a truth everywhere present in Hindu, Buddhist, and Jain ideas about karma, rebirth, and liberation: the gods themselves do not know about liberation, but will eventually have to be reborn as human to take the final steps in escaping the cycles of rebirth. They too will need to become, eventually, those creatures they see merely as "sacrificial animals."

38. The next series of verses praise the glories of Devanāyaka, in preparation for the formal prayers for mercy and the prayer of surrender, emphasizing the devotee-poet's utter helplessness (*akiñcanatvam*) in tones that strongly suggest the theology of the Teṉkalai Ācāryas.

39. This verse not only alludes to the famous passage in the *Bhagavad Gītā* (IX: 26) about the merit of the simplest acts of devotion but also refers to the traditional perils associated in orthodox Vedic ritual with rites left incomplete, undone, in error. Here, the simplest action in the name of the personal Lord is efficacious.

40. This line plays on various forms of the word *prasāda*, grace: *apasāe apasaṇṇā tujjha pasāyammi dāsasacca pasaṇṇā* (Skt: *aprasāde aprasannāḥ tava prasāde dāsasatya prasannāḥ*).

41. In Indian folklore the *cātaka* bird cannot drink directly from normal sources of water because of a hole in its throat; to get water it needs the rain so it can take the water in directly through its upturned open beak. Thus, its proverbial thirst in literature.

42. Here begins a powerful string of penitential verses work to reduce the role of human effort in the action of grace and salvation, down "almost to zero." See discussion in *Singing the Body of God*, Conclusion, 235–236.

43. This alludes to the notion of the "accidental good deed" (*yādṛcchikasukṛta*) that, in Veṅkaṭeśa's theology, Vishnu is always fervently on the lookout for. Here, the poet can't even seem to manage this most open of possibilities in the action of salvation. Like the Teṉkalais, Veṅkaṭeśa emphasizes here in the emotional space of the poem the utter dependance of the soul on God's grace—its own effort (its smallest "gesture" that inspires in God a pretext [*vyāja*] for salvation) is seemingly useless.

44. Again, here is a potent image of utter helplessness and the lack of a meaningful human gesture in the economy of salvation. This is the most extreme depiction of the divided heart, asymmetry in the religious drama of lover and beloved. For a general discussion of salvation in Veṅkaṭeśa *the poet* and in his Teṉkalai opponents, see *Singing the Body of God*, chapter 6: 175–180.

45. This negative image of the body is quite common in Teṉkalai writings, and relatively uncommon in Veṅkaṭeśa. See especially the *Ārtiprabandham* of Maṇavāḷamāmuni (verse 33), in Amaladass, *Deliver Me, My Lord*, 70–71. This is one of many examples of Teṉkalai-like imagery in these penitential verses. Veṅkaṭeśa the poet creatively appropriates the voices of his opponents in the emotional and existential experience of the poem (while reserving important theological scruples for the philosophical and theological/commentarial venues of his prose work).

46. Note that the parent-child metaphor has for the moment replaced that of the lover-beloved or the master-slave. The last verse of the *śatakam* will juxtapose both parent-child and lover-beloved attitudes to God. In the next set of verses the poet prays to ascend to heaven in a glorious body of "spiritual matter" (*suddhasattam*; Skt: *śuddha sattvam*) and become a *nityasūri*, one of the celestial angels that surround the figure of Vishnu in heaven. The *nityasūris* are "angelic icons" in that they are identical to Vishnu in every attribute but the power to create and destroy.

47. Veṅkaṭeśa alludes here to the almost Dantean journey after death with different gods, beginning with Agni and ending with the Lord of Lightning, meeting the soul on different stages of its journey upward.

48. "eternal lovely body of light": *suddhasattamayasommataṇum*.

49. The Viraja River borders the created worlds and the worlds of heaven (Vaikuṇṭha) in Vaiṣṇava cosmology.

50. This last phrase, one long compound in the original modifying *payapayume* (Skt: *padmapade*), is a remarkable example of alliteration (*anuprāsa*) and concision: *mayaṇariyu-mayuḍamaṇḍaṇa-surasariyāsottasūiya-mahuppavahe*, and in Skt: *madanaripu-makuṭamaṇḍana-surasaritsrotassūcita-madhupravāhe*. See also the image of the toes spilling the Gaṅgā in *Devanāyakapañcāśat*, above.

51. "like . . . your angelic icons": *tuha . . . sūrisariccho*.

52. "equal to you, if only in pleasure": *appasamabhoyamettam* (Skt: *ātmasamabhogamātram*). Devotees are able to share in the Lord's pleasure, though they of course are not equal in power and so on. Here there is a mutual enjoyment: Vishnu enjoys his companions on earth in the same measure that they enjoy him. After spending

several verses extolling the voyage away from this earth and this existence—the escape to heaven—the poet suddenly shifts perspective. Veṅkaṭeśa here praises the earthly *līlā* or divine "play" of Vishnu on earth (as an *avatāra*) over *mokṣa* (liberation) itself. He desires to return, to be reborn again, to experience the earthly bliss of the divine by being one of Vishnu's blessed companions. Both values—that of the divinized earth and of nonreturn and the eternal bliss of heaven—operate in creative juxtaposition in Veṅkaṭeśa's hymns.

53. These images beg the question of self-effort, leaving us with very little *vyāja* to go on. Veṅkaṭeśa reaches deep into the "almost zero" in this verse. Such infant-mother images are also quite common in Teṉkalai writings on surrender.

54. Strictly speaking, here is the verse that would serve as the *vyāja* or "pretext" in Veṅkaṭeśa's philosophical sense of the term.

55. "elegant": *suhayam* (Skt: *subhagam*), also "well made, attractive"; "filled with all fine qualities": *samaggaguṇam* (Skt: *samagraguṇam*), "filled with virtues, qualities"; "in the hearts of the connoisseurs": *sahiyayahiyaesu* (Skt: *sahṛdayahṛdayeṣu*), literally, "in the hearts of the good-hearted." *Sahṛdaya* also means one who is sympathetic; in poetics it means the "connoisseur," the person of taste and "sensibility"—the one who really understands, who is sympathetic to the subtle resonances of fine poetry.

56. See the brief but perceptive discussion of Prākrit *āryā* meter in Selby, *Grow Long, Blessed Night*, 83–84.

57. See her "Afterword" to *The Absent Traveller*, 71–81. This is a translation of verses from the great Māhārāṣṭrī anthology, the *Gāthāsaptaśatī* (the *Sattasāī*), dated ca. 200–450 C.E., attributed to Hāla, the Sātavāhana king. For a survey of Prākrits in the history of Indian literature, see Warder, *Indian Kāvya Literature*, I:5–8. For a general study of the *Sattsāī*, see Dundas, *The Sattasaī and Its Commentators*; for a detailed study of the *Sattasāī* and its relationship to Tamil and Sanskrit, see Hart, *The Poems of Ancient Tamil*. For a fascinating look at Sanskrit commentaries on the *Sattasāī*, see Selby's article "Desire for Meaning." Mahārāṣṭrī, as a cultivated literary dialect used for literature, and not in daily speech, is very much like the Provençal (Occitan) literary language of the troubadours. See Blackburn, *Proensa*.

58. See *Singing the Body of God*, 215–231.

59. See Introduction, above, "At the Edge of the Woods: Thoughts about Translation," and Smith, "A Twice-Told Tale," in *Relating Religion*, 362–374; here esp. 371–372.

CHAPTER 6

1. The text is taken from *Śrīdeśikastotramālā*, Sanskrit text with Tamil commentary by V. N. Śrīrāmatēcikācāryar, 637–657.

2. "Cherished lover of simple cowherd girls": *vallavījanavallabham*, a phrase with a certain alliterative charm. This phrase is also said to point to Krishna's *sauśīlya* or "gracious condescension."

3. *Jayantīsaṃbhavam*: I have expanded this phrase for clarity and detail, following the commentators. "Jayantī" is an astrological conjunction that can be described with

some poetic grace. Rāmatēcikācāryar's Tamil gloss describes Jayantī as the time when "the constellation Rōhiṇī is united with the eighth day of the dark of the moon in the month of Siṃha Śrāvaṇa, or Āvaṇi"; *jayantī eṇpatu simha crāvaṇa (āvaṇi) māttatil kiruṣṇapakṣattu aṣṭamiyuṭaṉ cērukiṉra rōhiṇī nakṣtra mātum.* This descriptive epithet is said to refer to Krishna's *saulābhyam* or "easy accessibility."

4. "luminous power" and "shining body" both translate the rich word *dhama,* meaning "majesty," "glory," "luminary," "effulgence," "power." I follow commentators in identifying this luminous power with the luminous body of the Lord Krishna that "moves about" or "wanders" in Vṛndāvana, implied in the phrase *vṛndāvanacaram* in the first *pada* of the verse. This can also imply the "feet" of the Lord. In Rāmatēcikācāryar's Tamil gloss, *dhama* is a kind of *jyoti* or radiant light, identified with Lord Krishna's "lovely body" (*vaṭivu*): *kaṇṇapirāṉeṉapatum oru cōti vaṭivai toḻukiṉrēṉ* (I adore/worship the lovely form/body, a radiant light that is called Lord Krishna). The mention of Vṛndāvana here is said to index Krishna's *vātsalyam,* "tender loving affection [of a cow for her calf]."

5. The image of Krishna as wearing the "victory" garland indexes his *svāmitvam,* his "independent mastery" or "supreme Lordship." The entire verse, in its simple compass, is said to embrace various attributes of Krishna, from the tender love of a mother or a lover, and easy accessibility, to supreme Lordship of the universe. The verse is also analyzed by commentators to include three major *rasas,* aesthetic "flavors" or experience, that are important to Krishna's "play" in the world: *śṛṅgāra,* the "erotic" (in the allusion to *gopīs*); *vīra* the "heroic," indicated by the *vaijayantī* garland; and *adbhūta* or "wonder," indexed by his "moving about" in the forests where, as we will see in the body of the *stotra,* he performs a variety of awesome feats of divine power. See Appayya Dīkṣita's commentary on this verse, where it also appears as the first verse of Veṅkaṭeśa's *Yadavābhyudayam.*

6. The identification of Veṅkaṭeśa himself with *vāc,* Speech (glossed here and in the commentaries as Sarasvatī), who "delights" (Tamil gloss *mukiḻ*) or "relishes" being on the very lap of the Lord, is a common one in praise-verses of the poet, and points to his eloquence and mastery of language.

7. *varṇatrikoṇarucire varapuṇḍarīke.*

8. *vallabacakravartī*: this verse has the flavor of a visualization used in ritual meditation of the Lord and his powers.

9. This descending, broken episodic phrase translates the first four padas of the verse, two long, elegant and alliterative compounds in Sanskrit: *āmnāyagandhiruditaspuritāgharoṣṭham āsrāvilekṣaṇam anukṣaṇamandahāsyam.*

10. *gopālaḍimbhavapuṣam.*

11. *prāṇastanandhayam.*

12. *param pumāṃsam,* glossed as the more common epithet, *parama puruṣa,* or "supreme person," a phrase that hearkens back to the Upaniṣads and the Bhagavad Gītā. This of course stresses the wonder of Krishna's play, which brings together opposing forms of the big and the little, the earthly and the cosmic, the awesome and powerful, and the tiny and vulnerable: Krishna is no less than the "Supreme Person" in the tiny body of an infant who cries and fusses and suckles, but when he

breathes one smells the fragrance of Vedas, and when the breasts he happens to suckle are those of the demon Pūtanā, he kills without mercy.

13. *anibhṛtābharaṇam*: "ornaments/jewels that tremble/move/stir." Tamil gloss: *aṇikaḷ acaiyappeṟṟatāy*. Because the dancing feet are being described, I take this reference to mean the anklets on the feet; see subsequent verses describing the rattling of jewels in anklets.

14. *dadhnā nimithamukhareṇa nibadhatālam*: a vivid, vigorous phrase, literally, "unrestrained/vigorous rhythms with noisy/talkative ('mouthy') churning of curds." I try in my translation to capture the clever use in this phrase of *mukhareṇa* (noisy/talkative, "mouthy") with and aural/audial and rather fanciful phrase "thwacking ruckus."

15. In the loping *mandākrāntā* meter*: hartum kumbhe vinihitakaraḥ svādu haiyaṅgavīnam.*

16. *īṣat pracalitapado nāpagacchan na tiṣṭhan*: "neither fleeing nor standing still, trembling just a little." The sense of the verse is that this god-child pretends to be frightened, or perhaps more accurately, "plays" (*līlā*) at being frightened.

17. *mithyāgopaḥ*: verses 3, 4 and 5 are all in the long-lined, loping, rhythmic *mandākrāntā* meter, suitable to its subject, the dancing and pranks of the child Krishna. I have tried, in my translation, mostly visually on the page, to reproduce this loping, shifting rhythm, in the spacing of broken words and phrases. See also verses 17–20.

18. *tat kimapi brahma*: literally, "that I-don't-know-what-kind of *Brahman*," a deceptively short phrase that appears in other *stotras* of Veṅkaṭeśa, where it is used to evoke the unknowable, inconceivable and "transcendent" ultimate reality of the Upaniṣads. The power of this verse, of course, lies in Veṅkaṭeśa's juxtaposition of this phrase with the erotic and maternal affective dimensions of this "lovable" *Brahman*.

19. *smarāmi*: "I remember, visualize," "I mediate on." A verb commonly used in texts describing devotional mediations/visualizations of the qualities of a god (or of the Buddha in a Buddhist context). To "remember" here is to evoke the meditative *presence*, the presentational reality, of the god or Buddha.

20. *niśāmayami nityam.*

21. *yamalārjunadṛṣṭabālakelim yamunāsākṣikayauvanam yuvanam.*

22. "joy and wealth": *sampadam.*

23. The original phrase contains, like so much of Veṅkaṭeśa's Sanskrit, some lovely music: *aruṇādharasābhilāṣavaṃśam.*

24. *bhajāmi.*

25. *karuṇām kāraṇamānuṣīm.*

26. *ajahadyauvanam.*

27. *karaṇonmādakavibhramam maho.*

28. "sweet reed flute": *manojñavaṃśanālaḥ*; Tamil gloss: *iṉiya kuḻaliṉ*. "Ecstasies": *vimoha*; Tamil: *mayakkam.*

29. "flood": *rasa*, water.

30. *harinīlaśilāvibhaṅganīlāḥ.*

31. "glorious visions": *pratibhāḥ*, "images," "appearances."

32. *akhilān . . . kālān*: "at every moment/time/waking hour."

33. "beauty": *abhirūpyam.* Salvation and aesthetic beauty are deeply twined together in the poetics of Veṅkaṭeśa's *stotras.* Cf. *Singing the Body of God,* 101–109, 130–133, 195–197, 238–239.

34. *abhilāpakramadūram:* "far beyond the scope of my words/language/expression."

35. *hṛdi . . . likhitaḥ kena mamaiṣa śilpinā*: "young man," literally youth, *yuvā,* a common word used, and played upon, in these verses.

36. *madanātura.*

37. *añcanam;* "collyrium, / eye-black," often compared to the shiny blue-black body of Vishnu/Krishna in Veṅkaṭeśa's *stotras.*

38. "breathes in tune": literally, *bhāṣita,* which "speaks" in unison with (the bangles). The stanza plays with the sounds of the consonant cluster *añj*—in *añjalī,* the greeting/salute with hands pressed; *mañju,* lovely, charming; and *añjanam,* meaning *kohl*—to mime the threshing sound of the jeweled anklets.

39. Again, my English translation seeks to match the sounds of the original, here *śithilavalayaśiñja,* to mime the "slinking" sound of loose bangles on the dancing arms. The verse is in the long-lined, finely detailed, musical *mālinī* meter.

40. *lāṅgalī*: flowers from the sheaves of the coconut palm; Tamil: *tennampālai.*

41. *bandhujīva*: red hibiscus.

42. *guñjā*-beads: Tamil: *kuṉṟimaṇi.*

43. *kitavaḥ ko'pi.*

44. Verses 17–20 are composed in the rhythmic *mandākrāntā* meter, which slows the reader's eye and ear, suitable for these detailed "thick" descriptions of Krishna. See also verse 5, above.

45. *pulakarucire*: the shoulder of the lady "shines with horripilation." The lady/goddess here is identified in the commentaries as Nappiṉṉai, Vishnu/Krishna's Tamil wife/lover.

46. *gopakanyābhujaṅgaḥ.*

47. *Pratyālīḍa*-posture: the left foot forward, right backward, an attitude in archery. The context here is that she is making ready to shoot colored water from her "syringe" in the "water sports" of the *holī* festival, where devotees throw colors at one another.

48. "long syringe": *bhastrāyantra*: vessel, pouch (with bellows), or syringe filled with colored water.

49. *vārikrīḍa.*

50. *vallavīvallabho.* See verse 1.

51. *bhaktajīvātuḥ.*

52. Yamunā's epithet has a lovely musicality in the original: *dinakarasutāsaṃnidhau.*

53. *līlāsmero.*

54. *kāmī kaścit*: "what kind of (mysterious, unfathomable) lover/one in love." *Kāmī* here implies Krishna's twofold dimension as Beloved—the object of love—and one who is also *in* love.

55. *daivatam kimapi.*

56. *divyaveṇurasikam.*

57. For a longer version of this afterword, which includes a discussion of Veṅkaṭeśa's *mahākāvya* on the life of Krishna, the *Yādavābhyudayam,* along with an earlier version of a full translation of *Gopālaviṃśati,* see my "At Play in the Forests of the Lord."

58. See Dehejia, *Āṇṭāḷ and Her Path of Love,* 14–15.

59. For an elaborate argument for a specifically southern Tamil "Kṛṣṇaism" and its subsequent influence in the *Bhagavāta Purāṇa* and northern Krishna devotion, see Hardy, *Viraha-bhakti,* especially part 4, "Māyōṉ Mysticism: The Āḻvārs."

60. See Narayanan, *The Way and the Goal,* 25–26. Narayanan goes on to argue the importance of the figure of Rāma in Āḻvār devotion.

61. See Narayanan, *The Way and the Goal,* 106–112. See also, for this kind of layering where images of Rāma, Krishna, and other *avatāras* intermingle, the great Tamil praise-poem of Tiruppāṇāḻvār, the *Amalaṉātipiraṉ,* translated in *Singing the Body of God,* 141–144.

62. See full translation of poem and discussion in *Singing the Body of God,* 93–94. His other Tamil *prabandhams,* such as *Mummaṇikkōvai* and *Navamaṇimālai,* are strewn with references to Krishna mingled with other *avatāras,* all of which are present in his experience of the specific temple image being praised. See *Singing the Body of God,* chapter 4, "The Fruits of Mukunda's Mercy," 115–134, and the afterwords to the above two *prabandhams* in this volume.

63. From *Devanāyakapañcāśat* 27, cited in *Singing the Body of God,* 208–209, and in this volume.

64. See *Singing the Body of God,* Introduction and especially chapters 4 and 7, pp. 115–134 and 199–231.

CHAPTER 7

1. For a detailed reading of Parakāla's hagiographic sources, see Hardy, "The Śrīvaiṣṇava Hagiography of Parakāla."

2. For a thorough discussion of the classical Tamil landscapes, see Ramanujan, *Poems of Love and War,* 231–297, esp. the useful chart on 242. For specific references in Tirumaṅkaiyāḻvār, I have consulted the edition with commentary of Vīrarākavācāriyaṉ, the Visishtadvaita Pracharini Sabha edition, vol. 4 (1978), 295–308. For a comparative example of the devotional use of the *caṅkam* landscapes in the poems of the Tamil Śaiva saint-poets, see Peterson, "Singing of a Place."

3. We have already spoken of Veṅkaṭeśa's use of Tirumaṅkaiyāḻvār's epithet *Aṭiyavarkku meyyaṉē* (The Lord of Truth to His Servants). See Hardy, *Viraha-bhakti,* 270–280 for a discussion of the basic thematic elements of Āḻvār poems, both overall and in each stanza.

4. Parakāla is also known for his creative use of folk materials and his remarkable (and unique) *maṭal* poems that describe the defiant girl-in-love parading her pain (born of separation from her beloved) in the streets, "riding the palmyra horse."

See Hardy, *Viraha-bhakti*, 388–402. Archana Venkatesan is currently working on a long-term project that looks at the *maṭal* poems and their devotional motifs. For the Tamil texts, with modern Tamil word glosses and commentaries, see the *Ciṟiya Tirumaṭal* and the *Periya Tirumaṭal* in the collected works of Tirumaṅkaiyāḻvār, with Tamil commentary of Śrī Uttamur Vīrarākavācāriyaṉ, vol. 11, 77–146.

5. Such structures include the theological mediation of the Ācāryas, the salvific power of the communitiy of bhaktas, and an elaborated, ideologically pointed literature on the benefits of specific sacred places. See Hardy, *Viraha-bhakti*, 471.

6. *cerunti nāṉ malar: cerunti:* hound's berry, sedge, golden-flowered pear. Also *vāṭakōrai or curapuṉṉai* (*Calophylum Longifolium*). The commentator identifies this flowering tree as having the "qualities of *kuriñci*."

7. *ceyyavaḷ*: also "red" or "fair" lady.

8. *iṭam*: introducing a long compact description of place. This use of *iṭam* structures each verse (*tirumoḻi*), dividing it into two parts.

9. *teṉṉa eṉṉu vaṇṭu iṉ icai mural taru.*

10. *mātavi* or the *gurukkatti* is a form of jasmine, and so related, the commentator says, to the *mullai tiṇai* or "jasmine landscape" of *caṅkam* Tamil.

11. *aṭiyārkku meyyaṉ ākiya tevanāyakaṉ*: origin of the epithet favored by Veṅkaṭeśa in his Tamil poems to this same form of Vishnu. We have already seen how *mey* means both "body" and "truth."

12. *tikaḷ taru:* "gives splendor."

13. *ceyya tāmarai.*

14. *mullai am koṭi āṭa.*

15. *moykoḷ mātavi ceṇpakam:* the jasmine, *mātavi*, and champak flowers also signal for the commentator the *mullai tiṇai.*

16. *iṉ aruḷ*. This refers to the story of Narasiṃha, Prahlāda, and his even demon-father Hiraṇyakaṣīpu.

17. *eḻil tikaḷ:* "sheds beautiful luster."

18. *cēṟa koṇṭa taṇ paḻaṉmatu:* the commentator links these images to the *neytal tiṇai.*

19. *maṇi nīḻal:* "dark-jeweled/sapphire shade."

20. *miṭaintu:* "being thick-pressed; crowded; closely placed."

21. *poṇmalar tikaḷ.*

22. In commentary, this wild food is compared to the god and goddess, Perumaḷ joined with Periyapirāṭi. In a common allegorical move, the monkeys are the devotees, "servants" of the god and goddess.

23. Kino: *vēṅkai*; red cottonwood: kōṅku; champak: *ceṇpakam.*

24. *ulāviya*: "wandering," "moving about," rambling," used in initial rhyme at the beginning of each verse line.

25. *maṇi varai nīḻal*: this verse, according to the commentator, embodies *marutam tiṇai.*

26. *virai kamaḻntu mel karum kuḻal.*

27. *taṭam ār.*

28. *varai vaḷam tikaḻ:* "lustrous/shining with abundance of mountains."

29. *aṇai ceḻunati vayal [puku]*: this image of paddy fields (*vayal*) and rivers overflowing banks, according to the commentator, is an index to *marutam tiṇai.*

30. *akila.*

31. *kōl koḷ kai talattu.*

32. *vēl koṇ kai talattu*: initial rhyme with "our great father" who took in his hands the whip, above.

33. *pāvu taṇ tamiḻ.*

34. *mēvu cōtiyai*: "desired, delectable, refulgent, light."

Glossary

Ācārya: sectarian teacher/philosopher, distinguished in the Tamil traditions from Āḻvārs; scholar-preceptor of Śrīvaiṣṇava tradition. Veṅkaṭeśa is one of the great ācāryas of northern (Vaṭakalai) Śrīvaiṣṇavism.

Acyuta (Prākrit, Accua): name of Vishnu-Krishna, meaning "one who does not fall down," "one who does not stumble," "invincible."

Āgama: texts detailing ritual worship, generally to Vishnu or Śiva. The Pāñcarātra Āgamas are important ritual texts in Veṅkaṭeśa's Śrīvaiṣṇava tradition.

Agastya: a Vedic Seer who, in Tamil sources, is said to have spread the Vedic traditions in south India.

Ahalyā: "unploughable," the adulterous wife of the sage Gautama who was cursed by the sage to become a stone. Rāma freed Ahalyā from her stone-form with the touch of his foot.

akam: "interior," in ancient Tamil love poetry *akam* poems are poems of love that speak of various personae, mostly women, such as the heroine, the friend, or foster-mother. One of the two major genres of Tamil poetry, along with *puṟam*, the poems of war.

Āl̲vār: one of the Hindu saint-poets who flourished in the Tamil-speaking south of India from the sixth to the ninth centuries C.E. Their ecstatic songs are still popular among members of the Śrīvaiṣṇava community. They are central in temple worship and in household and private devotions.

aṃśa: an incarnation of a deity that embodies a portion or aspect of their powers. Veṅkaṭeśa is sometimes viewed as an *aṃśa* of Vishnu, as is Rāmānuja (see below, sv).

Ananta: also known as Śeṣa, the thousand-headed snake upon which Vishnu rests and/or sleeps as he reclines on the Ocean of Milk. Also a name of Krishna meaning "without limit."

an̲pu: love, tender affection, erotic love.

anubhava: "experience," "enjoyment," "relish." This term is used in Śrīvaiṣṇava literature both for commentary and also to name the limb-by-limb sensuously charged descriptions of the body of Vishnu.

arcā: "what can be worshiped." Vishnu enshrined in image form in Śrīvaiṣṇava temples.

arcāvatāra: a "descent" of Vishnu in a form that can be worshiped. One of the five forms of Bhagavān (the Lord) in the Pāñcarātra Āgamas.

aruḷ: "grace," mercy, even compassion in some texts. The Tamil term has many resonances, evoking meanings of becoming present, alive, close; here "grace" and mercy is almost the becoming material, the manifestation of an invisible spiritual principle; "emerging presence."

Āryāvarta: region of north India encompassing some of the major sacred sites, such as Vāraṇāsī. Veṅkaṭeśa is said to have taken a pilgrimage to the north and (as a southern ācārya) found it wanting.

ātman: lit: "self/oneself"; it can also mean "body." In the Upaniṣads, *atman* or Self is the supramundane, one, formless reality or ground of being inhering in every thing.

avatāra: an incarnation or "descent" of Vishnu, who periodically descends into this world to protect dharma (righteousness), according to the needs of time and place. Rāma and Krishna are two major *avatāras* of Vishnu. The classical number of *avatāras* is ten.

Balarāma: "he who delights in power," the elder brother of Krishna who has his own rich folklore, narrative, and ritual traditions in north India.

Bhagavān: the Lord, a title used in premodern India for both Vishnu and the Buddha; literally, "one possessing *bhaga*"—prosperity, dignity, distinction, excellence, majesty.

bhakta: "devotee," one who is devoted, who is a lover of god.

bhaktiyoga: the discipline (*yoga*) of devotional mediation, involving detailed study of Vedic texts and various ritual manuals, available only to male members of the upper three classes. One of two paths in Veṅkaṭeśa's Śrīvaiṣṇava community, the difficult one; the other is *prapatti* or *śaraṇāgati*, ritual "surrender."

Bhū/Bhūdevī: goddess of earth, one of two major consorts of Vishnu, along with Lakṣmī/Śrī.

Brahmā: the four-headed creator god, himself created by Vishnu. At the beginning of every new world-age, Brahmā emerges from a lotus sprung from the navel of Vishnu as he reclines on Śeṣa on the Ocean of Milk.

Brahman: originally, in Vedic ritual tradition, a term that referred to prayer-formulas and their powers to embody their referents, prayer and its power; in the Upaniṣads it becomes a name for absolute truth, ground of being, the substratum of the real. In a key Upaniṣadic formula, *atman* and *Brahman* are one.

cakra: the discus, one of Vishnu's weapons, along with the conch shell.

cakravāka: birds said to lament for their mates at night when they are separated; it is also said that the *cakravāka* bird has a hole in its throat, and so it needs the rain to drink. The thirst of the *cakravāka* bird is a common motif in Sanskrit love poetry.

Caṇḍāla: an outcast.

Cāṇūra: the wrestler who fought with Krishna.

Carama-śloka: the *Bhagavad Gītā*'s "last verse" (18:66), regarded as one of the esoteric teachings/"secrets" (*rahasya*) of Śrīvaiṣṇava literature.

Daitya: a son of Diti, a demon.

dānava: a class of demons.

darśana: "seeing"; "view"; devotional seeing; *darśana* goes both ways: it is seeing and being seen by the god.

dāsa: servant, slave. In Tamil *toṇṭai*, "slave," commonly used to refer to devotees of Vishnu.

dayā: mercy, compassion; an attribute of Vishnu, sometimes seen by Veṅkaṭeśa as a separate goddess.

Devakī: Krishna's mother.

Devanāyaka at Tiruvāhīndrapuram: "Lord of Gods in the Town of the Serpent King," a form of Vishnu in a village near Cuddalore on the eastern coast of Tamil Nadu where Veṅkaṭeśa lived for thirty years. He composed some of his most erotically charged poems (in Tamil and Sanskrit) to this particular form of Vishnu.

deva: a class of gods, antagonists of the *asuras*, a class of powerful "demons."

Devī: the essential form of the goddess, of which Durgā and Lakṣmī/Śrī are forms.

dharma: ritual, duty, righteousness, rule, law, virtue, norms of social and ritual action. A central concept in Hindu tradition and in Veṅkaṭeśa's Śrīvaiṣṇava community.

divya-deśa: a "sacred place," any one of the 108 sacred places in Śrīvaiṣṇava tradition. Tiruvahīndrapuram is one of these.

Dvārakā: Krishna's city on the Arabian Gulf.

Gajendra: an elephant devotee of Vishnu who was rescued by the Lord from the clutches of an alligator. Gajendra's story emphasizes the immediate, spontaneous grace of the Lord.

Gaṅgā: the sacred river of Vāraṇāsī, in Vaiṣṇava sacred narratives said to have emerged from the toenail of Vishnu.

Garuḍa: a huge eagle, devotee, and mount of Vishnu.

Gokula: a place near Vṛdāvana, the "forest of Vṛndā" where Krishna spent his childhood.

gopa: a male cowherd.

gopī: a female cowherd.

Govardhana: the hill that Krishna held up with his little finger to shelter a whole village from the rains of Indra.

Govinda: "cow-finder/tender," a name of Krishna.

guṇas: "strands" or "qualities" inherent in all matter, interwoven like strands of rope or thread. They are *sattva*, "goodness," "clarity, "light/lightness"; *rajas*, "dust," "passion," "action"; and *tamas*, "darkness," "inertia," heaviness.

guru: "heavy," a religious preceptor/teacher.

Hanumān: a monkey devotee of Rāma in the epic *Rāmāyaṇa* who is the paradigmatic servant of god; also known as Maruti.

Hari: name of Krishna meaning one who takes away evil, sin.

Hārda: the presence of the deity in the heart of the devotee. One of the five manifestations of Vishnu in Śrīvaiṣṇava theology.

Hiraṇyakaśipu: "having golden garments," Vishnu's demon antagonist in the Man-Lion (Narasiṃha) *avatāra* narratives. Twin brother of Hiraṇyākṣa and father of Prahlāda.

Hṛṣīkeśa: "Lord of the Senses," or "One with Bristling Hair," epithet of Krishna.

Indra: god of rain; king of the Gods.

iṉpam: Tamil, "sweetness"; also sexual enjoyment.

Janārdhana: a name of Krishna or Vishnu meaning "one who stimulates men."

Kali Yuga: the Kali or present world age, the last and most degenerate of the four world ages.

Kalikaṉṟi: a name of the great Āḻvār saint-poet Tirumaṅkaiyāḻvār.

Kalkin: "impure," name of the last *avatāra* of Vishnu; he rides a horse, and will usher in the end of the age.

Kalpavṛkṣa, Kalpaka, or Kalpataru: "wish-granting tree" of the gods. Veṅkaṭeśa likes to compare Vishnu to the "wish-granting tree" of heaven.

Kāma: Kāmadeva, the god of love who pierces his victims with flowery arrows of love; the term also denotes desire, lust, sensual enjoyment, pleasure, one of the four aims of human life (*puruṣārtha*) in Hindu dharma tradition.

Kaṃsa: king of Mathurā, uncle and sworn enemy of Krishna. Krishna ultimately leaves the pastoral bliss of Vṛdāvana to go to Mathurā to kill Kaṃsa.

Kaṇṇaṉ, Kaṇṇā: "dear one," Tamil name of Krishna in Āḻvār poetry and in the Tamil *prabandhams* of Veṅkaṭeśa.

karma: *viṉai* in Tamil, "work," "act," "action" and the reaction generated from it. Karma binds a being to the cycle of births and deaths and, in Veṅkaṭeśa's Śrīvaiṣṇava theology, can only be cut off by the grace of Śrī and Vishnu.

Kātyāyanī: a name of the goddess associated with women's rites for fertility and love. The *gopīs* were worshiping this goddess early one morning in the local village tank when Krishna stole their clothes.

Kaustubhā: jewel obtained from the churning of the Ocean of Milk, worn by Vishnu-Krishna.

kāvya: classical Sanskrit literary art, including both lyric poetry and drama.

Keśava: name of Krishna, one who has (beautiful) "hair."

Keśī: horse demon sent to kill young Krishna.

kṛṣṇa: literally, "black," "dark one"; in Tamil, Māyōṉ; Krishna, *avatāra* of Vishnu.

Kubjā: "hunch-backed," a hump-backed girl straightened by Krishna.

Kūrma: "tortoise," the toroise *avatāra* of Vishnu, one of the ten *avatāras* of the god.

Lakṣmī: Śrī, the goddess of good fortune, splendor, and the auspicious, born in the churning of the Milk Ocean; wife of Vishnu.

līlā: "sport," "play," Krishna's sports or pastimes when he incarnates into the world; *līlā* can also evoke games or sexual play.

Mādhava: tribal name of Vishnu-Krishna; "descendant of Madhu."

Madhusūdana: "killer of Madhu," the demon "spring."

maṇipravāḷa: "jewels and coral"; term denoting a hybrid language mixing Sanskrit and a vernacular, such as Malayāḷam or Tamil. A Sanskrit-Tamil *maṇipravāḷa* is used by the Śrīvaiṣṇava theologians in their commentaries on the poems of the Tamil saints.

Mathurā: Krishna's birthplace, near Vṛndāvana.

Matsya: the "fish" *avatāra* of Vishnu.

Māyā: "power," wizardry, "brilliance," covering/illusion; "astonishing, wonderful, deceitful" power; the power of a god, often symbolized by the goddess.

Meru: the golden mountain rising at the center of the earth and abode of gods.

Mukunda: name of Vishnu meaning "giver of liberation."

mūrti: "form," image; the temple icon that, in the visionary experience of Veṅkaṭeśa, in his "devotional eye," is a living body of the god.

Nammāḻvār: The most famous and revered of the Tamil saint-poets whose cycle of poems to Vishnu, the *Tiruvāymoḻi*, is compared by the commentators to the temple images of Vishnu himself.

Nārāyaṇa: a name for Vishnu, especially during the period of dissolution at the end of a world-age. "Son of man," "son of the waters," a very important epithet in the Pāñcarātra Āgamas.

Nṛsiṃha: half-man, half-lion *avatāra* of Vishnu, who saved the child devotee Prahlāda from Hiraṇyakaśipu, his murderous father.

Oṃ: sound representation of *Brahman*, the ground of being. As threefold AUM, the syllable respresents external world of forms, internal world of dreams/dream images, and dreamless sleep.

Pāñcarātra: "five nights," ritual texts that detail Vaiṣṇava worship and practice and were formative in shaping liturgies of Śrīvaiṣṇava temples in Tamil Nadu.

Parāśurāma: "Rāma with the Axe," the *avatāra* of Vishnu who exterminated the warrior classes twenty-one times, a fierce form of Vishnu.

Pārijāta: The coral tree, a celestial tree whose fragrant flowers never fade.

prabandham: "work," composition; classical Tamil poetic form; there are ninety-six types of *prabandham*.

Prahlāda: "joyful excitement," a great child devotee who survived various attempts on his life by his violent father, Hiraṇyakaśipu, by simple, passionate appeal to Lord Vishnu.

Pralambāsura: a demon who infiltrated Vraj in the guise of a cowherd boy.

pūjā: honor, worship, ritual hospitality; prestations in honor of temple images.

Pūtanā: "stinking," a demoness who is said to cause diseases in children, and who takes the form of a beautiful woman who tries to kill Krishna by offering the child milk from her breasts that had been smeared with poison. Krishna ended up by sucking the very life-breath out of the demoness through the milk in her breasts.

puṟam: "outer," "exterior," old Tamil term for poems of war and heroism. One of two genres of classical Tamil poetry, the other being *akam*, "interior" poems of love. Veṅkaṭeśa, and the Āḻvārs before him, used both genres, often mixing them together, in poems in praise of Vishnu as god-king and lover.

Rāma: *avatāra* of Vishnu who rescued his wife Sītā after she was kidnapped by the demon-king Rāvaṇa. The Sanskrit *Rāmāyaṇa* is one of many *Rāma-kathās,* stories of Rāma, a narrative tradition that still flourishes today in various Indian languages, in folk, ritual, and literary traditions.

Rāmānuja: the eleventh-century Vaiṣṇava theologian of Viśiṣṭādvaita Vedānta, so-called "qualified non-dualism," who is considered the most important ācārya or teacher/preceptor in the Śrīvaiṣṇava community.

ratī: "love-play" or sexual pleasure; the wife of Kāma the love god.

Rāvaṇa: evil king of Laṅkā in the *Rāmāyaṇa* who abducted Rāma's wife Sītā.

Rōhiṇī: "red" or "red cow," a constellation.

sādhya-upāya: the way that has to be undertaken by a devotee, an aspirant to union with god. In Śrīvaiṣṇava theology, this refers to *bhaktiyoga,* and sometimes, most importantly, to *prapatti* or surrender.

śakti: "power," the active power of a deity associated with a wife/consort.

Sarasvatī: "flowing," name of a river-goddess associated with learning, the arts, music, and poetry; goddess of speech and wife of Brahmā; associated with Māhārāṣṭrī Prākrit, and also associated with the Milky Way in ancient Vedic traditions.

sāyujyā: "merging" with the Lord.

Śeṣa: "Ananta," the thousand-headed serpent upon which Vishnu reclines on the Ocean of Milk; incarnates as Krishna's brother Bālarāma.

siddha: a class of celestial or semi-divine beings; accomplished *yogīs* who have attained paranormal mystical powers, such as the ability to become infinitely small, light, great, to levitate, and so on.

siddha-upāya: the "accomplished way," the way as the goal itself, Vishnu.

śleṣa: double entendre; a figure of speech common in ornate Sanskrit poetry.

Śrī: "splendor," "radiance," "auspiciousness." The goddess as consort of Vishnu, Lakṣmī.

Śrīvaiṣṇava: a south Indian Hindu religious community that worships various forms of the god Vishnu and his consort Śrī, and accepts the Tamil songs of the Āḻvārs as equivalent to the Sanskrit Veda.

śrīvatsa: the mole and/or "mark" and its whorl of hair on the chest of Vishnu. I follow Tamil tradition in translating Śrīvatsa as a "mole" (*maccam or maru*), and not more generally as "mark."

stotra: "praise-poem," a major genre of Sanskrit devotional poetry.

Tiru: Tamil word for Śrī.

Tirumāl: Tamil term for Vishnu-Krishna, Holy Dark Lord. The other common epithet, sometimes used by Veṅkaṭeśa, is Māyōṉ, also "The Dark One."

Tiru-Pāṇ-Āḻvār: The "Holy Singer-Master," an eighth-century Untouchable saint-poet who lived near the great temple of Raṅganātha on the Kāvērī River in Trichy District, Tamil Nadu.

tulasī or *vṛndā*: a sacred plant, related to basil, sacred to Vaiṣṇavas and important adornment for icons of Vishnu-Krishna; a plant goddess.

Upaniṣads: ancient philosophical texts of the late Vedic period, key texts in the formation of the Vedānta schools.

vaijayantī: a type of never-fading flower used in Krishna's garland.

Vaikuṇṭha: the eternal abode of Vishnu, gained by the soul that has won liberation. Often Veṅkaṭeśa will say that he would prefer to be reborn here, on earth, near the earthly shrine of the Lord, than to go to Vaikuṇṭha: a fine way to praise the powerful presence of Vishnu for devotees in his earthly shrines and iconic forms.

Vaiṣṇava: a follower of Vishnu-Krishna.

Vāmana: dwarf *avatāra* of Vishnu.

Vanamālikā: garland of wild flowers that adorns the chest of Vishnu.

Varāha: boar *avatāra* of Vishnu who rescued the earth from the demon Hiraṇyākṣa.

Vāsudeva: name of Krishna as son of Vasudeva.

Vaṭakalai: the "northern" school of Śrīvaiṣṇavas that claims Veṅkaṭeśa as its founding Ācārya.

Vedānta: "end of the Vedas," one of the six schools of orthodox Hindu philosophy; based upon the teaching in the Upaniṣads, the *Bhagavad Gītā*, and the *Brahma-sūtra*. Systematizes teachings about *atman* (self), *Brahman* (ground of being), the nature of the material world, and the way to *mokṣa* or liberation from the cycle of births and deaths, *saṃsāra*.

Vedāntadeśika: "teacher of the Vedānta," the main title of Veṅkaṭanātha or Veṅkaṭeśa, a fourteenth-century south Indian poet, philosopher, and religious teacher in the Śrī Vaiṣṇava community of Tamil Nadu; a virtuoso poet-philosopher who wrote in Sanskrit, his native Tamil, and in southern Prākrit, an Indo-Āryan literary dialect related to Sanskrit.

viraha-bhakti: "love-in-separation"; the devotional attitude that emphasizes the "absent presence" of the god as divine Beloved; the pain of separation.

viṉai: "action," Tamil word for karma.

Viriñca: a name of the god Brahmā, the creator, perhaps from vi-$\sqrt{\text{rac}}$, to construct, contrive, fashion.

Vishnu: one who "spans," "stretches," "pervades;" all-pervasive. The preserver god, closely identified with Krishna, main deity of Śrīvaiṣṇavas, along with the goddess Śrī.

Vṛndāvana: "forest of *vṛndā*," the magical place where Krishna spent his childhood (see Gokula).

vyāja: "pretext," semblance. In his theological works, Veṅkaṭeśa emphasizes the necessity for a pretext in the economy of salvation—Vishnu needs something to go on, a lead, a pretext, to help the devotee to salvation. In his poems, on the other hand, he tends to emphasize the sheer grace of the god, giving salvation to the most unworthy of devotees, with a tender love "without pretext" (*avyāja vatsalya*).

vyūha: "form," "manifestation"; one of the four divine forms expanded from Vishnu in Pāñcarātra theology: Vāsudeva, Saṅkarṣaṇa, Pradyumna, and Aniruddha.

Yama: "twin" or "curb" or "bridle," Hindu Lord of the dead; he has a noose that he uses to drag sinners down to his hell.

Yamunā: river in Vṛndāvana.

Bibliography

WORKS OF VEṄKAṬEŚA

Acyutaśatakam. With the Prākrit commentary (*Prākṛta Prahriyā Vyākhyā*) by Deśikācārya, the Sanskrit commentary of Tātācārya, and the *maṇipravāḷa* commentary by Raṅganāthācārya. Edited by Tatācārya. Grantha and Tamil scripts. Kumbakonam, 1910, 1911.

Acyuta Satakam of Vedanta Desika. With meaning and commentary in English by D. Ramaswamy Iyengar. Madras: Sri Visishtadvaita Pracharini Sabha, 1983.

Devanāyakapañcāśat. With Sanskrit commentary of Rāghavācārya. Tamil trans. by Kitambi Rājagopālācārya. Grantha and Tamil scripts. Kumbakonam 1910.

Devanayaka Panchashat of Vedanta Desika. With meaning and commentary in English by D. Ramaswamy Ayyangar. Madras: A.T.M. Press, 1978.

Śrīdeśikastotramālā, uraiyuṭaṉ. Edited with a Tamil commentary of V. N. Śrīrāmatēcikācāryar. In one volume. [1966] Chennai: Lifco, 1982. The complete Sanskrit stotras of Veṅkaṭeśa with modern Tamil commentary.

Śrīmatvedāntadeśikagranthamālā. Edited by K.P.B. Aṇṇaṅkarācāriyar and Śrī Sampatkumārācāryasvāmin. In several volumes. 1940–1958. The collected Sanskrit works of Veṅkaṭeśa without commentary.

Śrītēcikappirapantam, uraiyuṭaṉ. Edited with Tamil commentary of Śrīrāmatēcikācāryar. [1944] Madras reprint, 1982. The complete Tamil *prabandhams* of Veṅkaṭeśa, with modern Tamil commentary.

Śrī Vedānta Deśika's Stotras (with English Translation) by Late Sriman S. S. Raghavan, Dr. M. S. Lakshmi Kumari, and Dr. M. Narasimhachary. C.I.T. Colony, Madras: Sripad Trust, 1995.

Varadarājapañcāśat, with Sanskrit Commentary bu Karūr Śrīnivāsācārya. Critically edited and translated into English by Pierre-Sylvain Filliozat. Bombay: Ananthacharya Indological Research Institute, 1990.

OTHER PRIMARY TEXTS

Kamparāmāyaṇam: Irāmāvatāram. Chennai: Kampaṉ Kaḻakam, 1984. Critical edition with no commentary.

Kuruparamparāpirapāvam [Skt: *Guruparamparāprabhāvam*] of Śrī Brahmatantra Svatantra Swāmi (the Vaṭakalai version). Madras: Lifco, 1968.

Nālāyira Tivviyappirapantam. Tamil works of the 12 Āḻvārs. Madras, 1987.

Nammāḻvār aruḷicceyta Tiruvāymoḻi. With Tamil commentary of Śrī Uttamur Vīrarākavācāriyaṉ. Seven volumes. Madras: Visishtadvaita Pracharini Sabha, 1985–1990; see for full English translation and commentary *Tiruvāymoḻi English Glossary* by S. Satyamurthi Ayyangar. Four volumes. Bombay: Ananthacharya Indological Research Institute, 1981.

Tirumaṅkaiyāḻvār aruḷicceyta Periyatirumoḻi. With Tamil commentary of Śrī Uttamur Vīrarākavācāriyaṉ. Ten volumes. Madras: Visishtadvaita Pracharini Sabha, 1977–1981. Volume 11 (1979) is entitled *Tirumaṅkaiyāḻvār arūḷicceyta ciṟiya tirumaṭal* and *periya tirumaṭal.*

OTHER SOURCES

Amaladass, Anand. *Deliver Me, My Lord. A Translation of Maṇavāḷamāmuni's Ārtiprabandham.* Delhi: Sri Satguru, 1990.

Āṇḍavān Svāmikaḷ, Śrī. Conversations with the author in Mylapore, Chennai (Madras), and in Sri Rangam, 1997–1998; correspondence, 1998–1999.

Barnstone, Willis. *The Poetics of Translation: History, Theory, Practice.* New Haven and London: Yale University Press, 1993.

Benjamin, Walter. "On Language as Such and on the Language of Man" [1916]. In *Reflections: Essays, Aphorisms, Autobiographical Writings,* edited with an introduction by Peter Demetz, 314–332. New York: Schocken, 1986.

———. "The Task of the Translator: An Introduction to the Translation of Baudelaire's 'Tableaux Parisiens.'" In *Illuminations,* edited with an introduction by Hannah Arendt, 69–82. New York: Schocken, 1969.

Blackburn, Paul, trans. *Proensa: An Anthology of Troubadour Poetry,* edited and introduced by George Economou. Berkeley: University of California Press, 1978.

Burrus, Virginia. "A Son's Legacy: Gregory of Nyssa." In *Begotten Not Made: Conceiving Manhood in Late Antiquity,* 80–133. Stanford: Stanford University Press, 2000.

Chakravarti, A. *Jaina Literature in Tamil.* With an introduction, footnotes, appendix, and index by K. V. Ramesh. New Delhi: Bhāratīya Jñānapīṭha, 1974.

Chitre, Dilip, trans. *Tukaram: Says Tuka.* Translated from the Marathi, with an introduction by Dilip Chitre. Delhi: Penguin, 1991.

Colas, Gérard. "Le dévot, le prêtre et l'image vishouite en Inde méridionale." In *L'image divine, culte et méditation dans l'Hindouisme. Études rassemblées par André Padoux*, 99–114. Paris: CNRS, 1990.

Cort, John E. "Elevating the Living Body of Sanskrit Poetry into American English." *Journal of South Asian Literature* 26.1–2 (1991): 44–76.

———, ed. *Open Boundaries: Jain Communities and Cultures in Indian History*. Albany: State University of New York Press, 1998.

Cutler, Norman. *Songs of Experience. The Poetics of Tamil Devotion*. Bloomington: Indiana University Press, 1987.

———. "Tamil Game Songs to Śiva." In *Religions of Indian in Practice*, edited by Donald S. Lopez, Jr., 145–158. Princeton: Princeton University Press, 1995.

Davis, Richard. *Lives of Indian Images*. Princeton: Princeton University Press, 1997.

———. "The Story of the Disappearing Jains: Retelling the Śaiva-Jain Encounter in Medieval South India." In John E. Cort, ed. *Open Boundaries*, 213–224. Albany: State University of New York Press, 1998.

Dehejia, Vidya. *Āṇṭāḷ and Her Path of Love: Poems of a Woman Saint from South India*. Albany: State University of New York Press, 1990.

———. "The Persistence of Buddhism in Tamil Nadu." *Mārg: A Magazine of the Arts* 39.4 (1998): 53–74.

Delmonico, Neil. "How to Partake in the Love of Kṛṣṇa." In *Religions of India in Practice*, edited by Donald S. Lopez, Jr., 244–268. Princeton: Princeton University Press, 1995. A translation of The *Govindalīlāmṛta* of Kṛṣṇadāsa Kavirāja.

Dharwadker, Vinay. *Kabīr: The Weaver's Songs*. New Delhi: Penguin India, 2003.

Dimock, Edward C., and Denise Levertov. *In Praise of Krishna: Songs from the Bengali*. Chicago: University of Chicago Press, 1967.

Doniger, Wendy, ed. *Purāṇa Perennis: Reciprocity and Transformation in Hindu and Jaina Texts*. Albany: State University of New York Press, 1993.

Dundas, Paul. *The Sattasaī and Its Commentators*. Turin: Publicazioni di Indologica Taurinensia, 1985.

Eck, Diana L. *Darśan: Seeing the Divine Image in India*. Second revised and enlarged edition. Chambersburg, Pa.: Anima, 1981.

Filliozat, Pierre-Sylvain. *Vedāntadeśika's Varadarājapañcāśat, with Sanskrit Commentary by Karūr Śrīnivāsācarya*. Critically edited and translated into English by P-S. Filliozat. Bombay: Ananthacharya Indological Institute, 1990.

Freedberg, David. *The Power of Images: Studies in the History and Theory of Response*. Chicago: University of Chicago Press, 1989.

Freeman, Rich. "Rubies and Coral: The Lapidary Crafting of Language in Kerala." *Journal of Asian Studies* 57.1 (February 1998): 38–65.

Fuller, C. J. *The Camphor Flame: Popular Hinduism and Society in India*. Princeton: Princeton University Press, 1992.

Gonda, Jan. *Eye and Gaze in the Veda*. Amsterdam-London: North-Holland Publishing Co., 1968.

———. *Medieval Religious Literature in Sanskrit*. Wiesbaden: Otto Harrasowitz, 1977.

———. *The Vision of the Vedic Poets.* The Hague: Mouton, 1963.

Gros, François, and T. V. Gopal Iyer, eds. *Tēvāram: Hymnes śaïvites du pays tamoul.* 2 vols. Pondicherry: Institut Français d'Indologie, 1984.

Handleman, Don, and David Shulman. *Śiva in the Forest of Pines: An Essay on Sorcery and Self-Knowledge.* Delhi: Oxford University Press, 2004.

Hardy, Friedhelm. "Information and Transformation—Two Faces of the Purāṇas." In *Purāṇa Perennis,* edited Wendy Doniger, 159–182. Albany: State University of New York Press, 1993.

———. "Mādhavendra Purī: A Link between Bengal Vaiṣṇavism and South Indian Bhakti." *Journal of the Royal Asiatic Society of Great Britain and Ireland* (1974, No. 1): 23–41.

———. "The Philosopher as Poet—A Study of Vedāntadeśika's *Dehalīśastuti.*" *Journal of Indian Philosophy* 7 (1979): 277–325.

———. *The Religious Culture of India: Love, Power, and Wisdom.* Cambridge: Cambridge University Press, 1994.

———. "The Śrīvaiṣṇava Hagiography of Parakāla." In *The Indian Narrative: Perspectives and Patterns,* edited by Christopher Shackle and Rupert Snell, 81–116. Wiesbaden: Otto Harrassowitz, 1992.

———. "TirupPāṇ-Āḻvār: The Untouchable Who Rode Piggy-Back on the Brahmin." In *Devotion Divine: Bhakti Traditions from the Regions of India. Studies in Honor of Charlotte Vaudeville,* edited by Diana L. Eck and Françoise Mallison, 129–154. Paris: École Française d'Extrême-Orient, 1991.

———. *Viraha-Bhakti: The Early History of Kṛṣṇa Devotion in South India.* Delhi: Oxford University Press, 1983.

Hart, George L. III. *The Poems of Ancient Tamil: Their Milieu and Their Sanskrit Counterparts.* Berkeley: University of California Press, 1975.

Hart, George L. III, and Hank Heifetz. *The Forest Book of the* Rāmāyaṇa *of Kampaṉ.* Translated, with annotation and introduction. Berkeley: University of Califronia Press, 1988.

Hawley, John Stratton. *Sūr Dās: Poet, Singer, Saint.* Seattle: University of Washington Press, 1984.

———. *Three Bhakti Voices: Mirabai, Surdas, and Kabir in Their Time and Ours.* Delhi: Oxford University Press, 2005.

Hawley, John Stratton, and Mark Juergensmeyer. *Songs of the Saints of India.* New York: Oxford University Press, 1988.

Heifetz, Hank, trans. *The Origin of the Young God. Kālidāsa's* Kumārasaṃbhava. Translated, with Annotation and an Introduction by Hank Heifetz. Berkeley and Los Angeles: University of California Press, 1985.

Heifetz, Hank, and Velcheru Narayana Rao, trans. *For the Lord of Animals: Poems from the Telugu. The* Kāḷahastīśvara Śatakamu *of Dhūrjati.* Berkeley: University of California Press, 1987.

Hopkins, Steven P. "At Play in the Forests of the Lord: The *Gopālaviṃśati.*" In *Sources of Krishna Tradition,* edited by Edwin Bryant (New York: Oxford University Press, 2007): 285–306.

———. "El símbolo, la palabra y el mito del pluralismo. Reflexiones sobre la metodología intercultural de R. Panikkar." *Anthropos. Revista de documentación científica de la cultural* 53–54 (1985): 79–86.

———. "Extravagant Beholding: Love, Ideal Bodies, and Particularity." In *History of Religions*, Vol. 47, No. 1 (August 2007): 1–50.

———. "In Love with the Body of God: Eros and the Praise of Icons in South Indian Devotion." *Journal of Vaiṣṇava Studies* 2.1 (Winter 1993): 17–54.

———. "Lovers, Messengers, and Beloved Landscapes: *Sandeśa Kāvya* in Comparative Perspective." *International Journal of Hindu Studies* 8.1–3 (2004): 29–55.

———. "Loving God in Three Languages: The Vedas of Vedāntadeśika." *Journal of Vaiṣṇava Studies* 10.2 (Spring 2002): 51–79. Special issue devoted to the work of John B. Carman.

———. "Singing in Tongues: Poems for Viṣṇu by Vedāntadeśika." *Journal of Vaiṣṇava Studies* 4.4 (Fall 1996): 159–187.

———. *Singing the Body of God: The Hymns of Vedāntadeśika in Their South Indian Tradition*. New York: Oxford University Press, 2002.

Hudson, Dennis. "*Āṇṭāḷ Āḻvār*: A Developing Hagiography." *Journal of Vaiṣṇava Studies* 1.2 (Winter 1993): 27–61.

———. *The Body of God: An Emperor's Palace for Krishna in Eighth-Century Kanchipuram*, edited by Margaret Case. New York: Oxford University Press, forthcoming.

———. "Bathing in Krishna: A Study in Vaiṣṇava Hindu Theology." *Harvard Theological Review* 73.3–4 (July–October 1980): 539–566.

Hulzsch, E. "The Ranganatha Inscription of Goppana: Śaka Saṃvat 1293." *Epigraphia Indica* VI. 7 (July 1901): 322–330.

Ingalls, Daniel H. H. *An Anthology of Sanskrit Court Poetry from Vidyākara's "Treasury."* Cambridge: Harvard University Press, 1979.

———. "A Sanskrit Poetry of Village and Field: Yogeśvara and His Fellow Poets." *Journal of the American Oriental Society* 74 (1954): 119–131.

Irshick, Eugene. *Dialogue and History: Constructing South India, 1765–1895*. Delhi: Oxford University Press, 1994.

Kane, P. V., and C. N. Joshi, eds. and trans. *The Uttararāmacarita of Bhavabhūti, with the Sanskrit commentary of Ghanaśyāma*. Delhi: Motilal Banarsidass, 1971.

Mariaselvam, Abraham. *The Song of Songs and Ancient Tamil Love Poems: Poetry and Symbolism*. Rome: Editrice Pontifico Istituto Biblico, 1988.

Mehrotra, Arvind Krishna. *The Absent Traveller: Prākrit Love Poetry from the Gāthāsaptaśatī of Sātavāhana Hāla*. Selected and translated by Arvind Krishna Mehrotra. Delhi: Ravi Dayal, 1991.

Merwin, W. S., and J. Moussaieff Masson, trans. *The Peacock's Egg: Love Poetry of Ancient India*. San Francisco: North Point Press, 1981.

Monius, Ann. *Imagining a Place for Buddhism: Literary Culture and Religious Community in Tamil-Speaking South India*. New York: Oxford University Press, 2001.

———. "The Many Lives of Daṇḍin: The Kāvyādarśa in Sanskrit and Tamil," *International Journal of Hindu Studies* 4.1 (April 2007): 1–37.

———. "U. Vē. Cāminātaiyar and the Construction of Tamil Literary 'Tradition.'" Paper given at the Conference on South Asia, Madison, Wisc., October 17, 1997.

Narayanan, Vasudha. "*Arcāvatāra*: On Earth as He Is in Heaven." In *Gods of Flesh, Gods of Stone*, edited by Joanne P. Waghorne, Norman Cutler, and Vasudha Narayanan, 53–66. Chambersburg, Pa.: Anima, 1985.

———. *The Vernacular Veda: Revelation, Recitation, and Ritual*. Columbia: University of South Carolina Press, 1994.

———. *The Way and the Goal: Expressions of Devotion in the Early Śrī Vaiṣṇava Tradition*. Washington, D.C.: Institute for Vaiṣṇava Studies, and Cambridge: Center for World Religions, Harvard, 1987.

Nayar, Nancy Ann. *Poetry as Theology: The Śrīvaiṣṇava Stotra in the Age of Rāmānuja*. Wiesbaden: Otto Harrassowitz, 1992.

———. *Praise-Poems to Viṣṇu and Śrī: The Stotras of Rāmānuja's Immediate Disciples*. Bombay: Ananthacharya Indological Research Institute, 1994.

———. "The Śrīvaiṣṇava Stotra: Synthesizing the Tamil and Sanskrit Vedas." *Journal of Vaiṣṇava Studies* 2.1 (Winter 1993): 55–77.

Orr, Leslie. "Jain and Hindu 'Religious Women' in Early Medieval Tamil Nadu." In *Open Boundaries: Jain Communities and Cultures in Indian History*, edited by John E. Cort, 187–212. Albany: State University of New York Press, 1998.

Panikkar, Raimundo. "El presente tempiterno: Una apostilla a la historía de la salvación y a la theología de la liberación." In *Teología y mundo contemporáneo: Homenaje a K. Rahner*, 133–175. Madrid: Ediciones Cristiandad, 1975.

———. *The Vedic Experience: Mantramañjarī. An Anthology of the Vedas for Modern Man and Contemporary Celebration*. Berkeley: University of California Press, 1977.

Parthasarathy, R., trans. *The* Cilappatikāram *of Iḷaṅkō Aṭikaḷ: An Epic of South India*. New York: Columbia University Press, 1993.

Peterson, Indira. *Poems to Śiva: The Hymns of the Tamil Saints*. Princeton: Princeton University Press, 1989.

———. "Singing of a Place: Pilgrimage as Metaphor and Motif in the Tēvāram Hymns of the Tamil Śaivite Saints." *Journal of the American Oriental Society* 102.1 (January–March 1982): 69–90.

———. "Śramaṇas against the Tamil Way: Jains as Others in Tamil Śaiva Literature." In *Open Boundaries*, edited by John Cort, 163–185. Albany: State University of New York Press, 1998.

Pollock, Sheldon. "The Cosmopolitan Vernacular." *Journal of Asian Studies* 51.1 (February 1998): 6–37.

———. "India in the Vernacular Millenium: Literary Culture and Polity, 1000–1500." *Early Modernities*, a special issue of *Daedalus: Journal of the American Academy of Arts and Sciences* (Summer 1998): 41–74.

———. "The Sanskrit Cosmopolis, 300–1300: Transculturation, Vernacularization, and the Question of Ideology." In *Ideology and Status of Sanskrit: Contributions to a History of the Sanskrit Language*, edited by Jan E. M. Houben, 197–247. Leiden: E. J. Brill, 1996.

———. "Three Local Cultures in the Sanskrit Cosmopolis (AD 300–1300)." Paper presented at a panel on "Contending with Languages in Pre-Modern India," American Association for Asian Studies Annual Meeting, Washington, D.C., April 6–9, 1995.

Prentiss, Karen Pechilis. *The Embodiment of Bhakti.* New York: Oxford University Press, 1999.

Rabin, Chaim. "The Song of Songs and Tamil Poetry." *Studies in Religion/Sciences Religieuses* 3.3 (1973–1974): 205–219.

Ramanujan, A. K. *Hymns for the Drowning: Poems for Viṣṇu by Nammāḻvār.* Princeton: Princeton University Press, 1981.

———. *Poems of Love and War, from the Eight Anthologies and the Ten Long Poems of Classical Tamil.* New York: Columbia University Press, 1985.

———. *Speaking of Śiva.* Baltimore: Penguin, 1973.

———. "Three Hundred *Rāmāyaṇas*: Five Examples and Three Thoughts on Translation." *Many Rāmāyaṇas: The Diversity of a Narrative Tradition in South Asia,* edited by Paula Richman, Berkeley: University of California Press, 1991: 22–49.

———. "Where Mirrors Are Windows: Toward an Anthology of Reflections." *History of Religions* 28.3 (February 1989): 187–216.

Ramanujan, A. K., Velcheru Narayana Rao, and David Shulman. *When God Is a Customer: Telugu Courtesan Songs by Kṣetrayya and Others.* Berkeley: University of California Press, 1994.

Ramaswamy, Sumati. "Language of the People in the World of Gods: Ideologies of Tamil before the Nation." *Journal of Asian Studies* 57.1 (February 1998): 66–92.

———. *Passions of the Tongue: Language Devotion in Tamil India.* Berkeley: University of California Press, 1997.

Rao, V. N. Hari. *History of Śrīrangam Temple.* Tirupati: Sri Venkatesvara University, 1976.

———. *Kōyil Oḻuku: The Chronicle of the Śrīraṅgam Temple with Historical Notes.* Madras: Rochouse and Sons, 1961.

Satyavrata Singh. *Vedānta Deśika. His Life, Works, and Philosophy.* Banaras: Chowkhamba Sanskrit Series, 1958.

Selby, Martha Ann. "Afterword" to *The Absent Traveller: Prākrit Love Poetry from Gāthāsaptaśatī of Sātavāhana Hāla,* selected and translated by Arvind Krishna Mehrotra, Delhi: Ravi Dayal, 1991: 71–81.

———. "Desire for Meaning: Providing Contexts for Prākrit *Gāthās.*" *Journal of Asian Studies* 55.1 (February 1996): 81–93.

———. *Grow Long, Blessed Night: Love Poems from Classical India.* New York: Oxford University Press, 2000.

Sells, Michael A. *Desert Traces: Six Classic Arabian Odes by 'Alqama, Shanfara, Labīd, 'Antara, Al-A'sha, and Dhu al-Rumma.* Middletown: Wesleyan University Press, 1989.

———. "Ibn 'Arabi's "Gentle Now, Doves of the Thornberry and Moringa Thicket." *Journal of the Muhyiddin Ibn 'Arabi Society* 10 (1991): 1–11.

———. *Stations of Desire: Love Elegies from Ibn 'Arabi and New Poems.* Jerusalem: Ibis Editions, 2000.

Shulman, David Dean. *The God on the Hill. Temple Poems from Tirupati by Tallapaka and Annamacarya.* Delhi: Oxford University Press, 2005.

———. *The King and the Clown in South Indian Myth and Poetry.* Princeton: Princeton University Press, 1985.

———. "Remaking a Purāṇa: The Rescue of Gajendra in Potana's Telugu Mahābhāgavatamu." In *Purāṇa Perennis: Reciprocity and Transformation in Hindu and Jaina Texts,* edited by Wendy Doniger, 212–273. Albany: State University of New York Press, 1993.

———. *Songs of the Harsh Devotee: The Tēvāram of Cuntaramūrttināyaṉār.* Philadelphia: Department of South Asia Regional Studies, 1990.

———, ed. *Syllables of Sky: Studies in South Indian Civilization in Honor of Velcheru Narayana Rao.* Delhi: Oxford University Press, 1995.

———. *Tamil Temple Myths: Sacrifice and Divine Marriage in the South Indian Śaiva Tradition.* Princeton: Princeton University Press, 1980.

———. *The Wisdom of Poets: Studies in Tamil, Telugu, and Sanskrit.* Delhi: Oxford University Press, 2001.

Smith, Jonathan Z. *Relating Religion: Essays in the Study of Religion.* Chicago: University of Chicago Press, 2004.

Soulen, Richard H. "The Waṣfs of the Song of Songs and Hermeneutic." *Journal of Biblical Literature* 86.2 (June 1967): 183–190.

Stein, Burton. *Peasant State and Society in Medieval South India.* Delhi: Oxford University Press, 1985.

———. "Social Mobility and Medieval South Indian Hindu Sects." In Stein, ed., *All the Kings' Mana: Papers on Medieval South Indian History.* Madras: New Era, 1984.

Steiner, George. *After Babel: Aspects of Language and Translation.* London: Oxford University Press, 1975.

———. *Real Presences.* Chicago: University of Chicago Press, 1989.

Trawick, Margaret. *Notes on Love in a Tamil Family.* Berkeley: University of California Press, 1990.

Twitchell, Chase, and Tony Stewart. *The Lover of God: Rabindranath Tagore's Vaiṣṇava Poems,* with introduction and postscript by Tony Stewart. Port Townsend, Wash.: Copper Canyon Press, 2003.

Varadachari, V. *Agamas and South Indian Vaisnavism.* Madras: Prof. M. Rangacharya Memorial Trust, 1982.

———. Correspondence and conversations with the author. Chennai (Madras), 1991.

———. *Two Great Acharyas: Vedanta Desika and Manavala Mamuni.* Madras: Prof. M. Rangacharya Memorial Trust, 1983.

Venkatachari, K.K.A. *The Maṇipravāḷa Literature of the Śrīvaiṣṇava Ācāryas: 12th to 15th Century A.D.* Bombay: Ananthacharya Indological Research Institute, 1978.

Waghorne, Joanne P., and Norman Cutler, with Vasudha Narayanan. *Gods of Flesh, Gods of Stone: The Embodiment of the Divinity in India.* Chambersburg, Pa.: Anima, 1985.

Warder, A. K. *Indian Kāvya Literature, Volume One: Literary Criticism*. Delhi: Motilal Banarsidass, [1972] 1989.

———. *Indian Kāvya Literature, Volume Two: Origins and Formation of the Classical Kāvya*. Delhi: Motilal Banarsidass, 1974.

Wilson, Francis. *The Love of Krishna: The* Kṛṣṇakarṇāmṛta *of Līlāsuka Bilvamaṅgala*, edited, with an introduction. Philadelphia: University of Pennsylvania Press, 1975.

Wimsatt, W. K., and Monroe C. Beardsley. *The Verbal Icon: Studies in the Meaning of Poetry*. Lexington: University Press of Kentucky, 1954.

Winternitz, M. *History of Indian Literature*. Vol. 3, Part 1. Translated by Subhadra Jhā. Delhi: Motilal Banarsidass, 1963.

Wulff, Donna. *Drama as a Mode of Religious Realization: The* Vidagdhamādhava *of Rūpa Goswāmī*. Chico, Cal.: Scholars Press, 1984.

Yocum, Glenn. *Hymns to the Dancing Śiva*. Columbia, Mo.: South Asia Books, 1982.

Young, Katherine. "Beloved Places (*Ukantaruḷinanilaṅkaḷ*): The Correlation of Topography and Theology in the Śrīvaiṣṇava Tradition of South India." Ph.D. dissertation, McGill University, 1978.

Zvelebil, Kamil. *Classical Tamil Prosody: An Introduction*. Madras: New Era, 1989.

———. *The Smile of Murugan. On Tamil Literature of South India*. Leiden: E.J. Brill, 1973.

Index